The Woke in the Age of Ego: Modern Arrogance and Ancient Warnings.

TABLE OF CONTENTS

INTRODUCTION: THE WOKE IN THE AGE OF EGO - A MODERN EPIDEMIC

Few threads in the tapestry of human history have been as persistent and influential as those of the ego. From the mythical fall of Icarus to the rise and fall of empires, the human ego has shaped our world in profound and often troubling ways. Yet, as we stand on the precipice of a new era defined by unprecedented technological advancement and global interconnectedness, we face a paradox. Despite our increased ability to understand and connect with one another, we seem more divided and self-centred than ever before.

This book, "The Woke in the Age of Ego: Modern Arrogance and Ancient Warnings," explores the pervasive influence of ego and arrogance in contemporary society. It draws parallels between our modern condition and the timeless wisdom found in biblical teachings. As we embark on this journey, we must define our terms and set the lens through which we will examine these complex issues.

In the context of this work, ego refers not merely to self-esteem or self-awareness but to an inflated sense of self-importance that often comes at the expense of others and the greater good. Arrogance, its close companion, is the overt expression of this inflated ego—a hubris that blinds individuals and institutions to their limitations and the valid perspectives of others.

Although the twin forces of ego and arrogance have always existed in human societies, our modern world has created a perfect storm for their proliferation. The instant gratification of social media, the cult of celebrity, the relentless pursuit of material wealth, and the increasing atomisation of communities have all contributed to what we might call an "ego epidemic."

As we delve into this topic, we will explore how this epidemic manifests in various sectors of society, from the halls of power in politics to the sterile corridors of healthcare institutions, from the glittering facades of consumer culture to the forefront of artificial intelligence research. We will see how unchecked ego and arrogance have led to decisions and systems that often prioritise individual or corporate gain over the common good in each arena.

But this book is not merely a critique of modern society. It is also an exploration of ancient wisdom, specifically the teachings and prophecies found in the Bible. Throughout history, religious texts have served as repositories of human experience and insight, offering guidance on the perennial challenges of human existence. With its rich tapestry of stories, proverbs, and prophecies, the Bible provides a particularly relevant lens through which to examine our current predicament.

From the Tower of Babel to the prophets' warnings against nations' arrogance, the Bible is replete with cautionary tales about the dangers of unchecked ego. These ancient writings, far from irrelevant in our technological age, offer timeless insights into the human condition and provide a moral compass for navigating the complexities of modern life.

As we progress through the chapters of this book, we will see time and again how scripture's warnings and wisdom align with the challenges we face today. This is not to suggest a simplistic or literal interpretation of biblical texts but rather to demonstrate the enduring relevance of these ancient insights when applied with nuance and context to our contemporary world.

Let us now preview the journey ahead, chapter by chapter, to understand the scope and structure of our exploration.

CHAPTER 1: THE FOUNDATIONS OF EGO IN MODERN SOCIETY

1. Introduction: The Rise of the Self

As we explore ego and arrogance in modern society, it is crucial to understand the historical and cultural foundations that have given rise to what we might call the "Woke in the Age of Ego." This chapter will trace the evolution of the concept of self and individuality from ancient times to the present day, focusing on the dramatic shifts in Western culture over the past few centuries.

The human ego is, in many ways, the story of human civilisation itself. Our understanding of the self has constantly evolved from the earliest myths and religious texts to the latest neuroscience and social media developments. Yet, as we will see, our society's current manifestation of ego is a unique and potentially troubling development in this long history.

To fully grasp the nature of our modern predicament, we must examine the interplay of a range of factors: philosophical ideas, technological advancements, economic systems, and social structures. These elements have shaped our understanding of the self and its place in the world.

As we continue, we will also consider how these developments align with or diverge from the teachings found in the Bible and other ancient wisdom traditions. This juxtaposition of modern trends with timeless insights will provide a framework for critically examining our current situation and considering potential paths forward.

2. The Ancient Roots of Ego

To understand the modern concept of ego, we must first look back to its ancient roots. The idea of the self, or the individual consciousness distinct from others and the world around it, has been the subject of philosophical and religious inquiry for millennia.

Ancient Greek philosophy explored the concept of self early. Socrates' famous dictum, "Know thyself," recognised individual consciousness and the importance of self-reflection. Plato's theory of the tripartite soul—divided into reason, spirit, and appetite—suggested a complex understanding of human psychology and the internal conflicts that can arise within an individual.

Meanwhile, ancient Eastern traditions take a different approach to the self-concept. Buddhist philosophy, for instance, posits the idea of "anatta" or "no self," suggesting that the notion of a fixed, unchanging self is an illusion. This starkly contrasts stern notions of individuality and has profound implications for how one might approach the idea of the ego.

The Judeo-Christian tradition, which forms the backdrop for much Western culture, offers a nuanced approach to the self. On one hand, it strongly emphasises individual moral responsibility and the unique value of each human soul. On the other hand, it repeatedly warns against pride and self-aggrandisement, epitomised in sayings such as "Pride goes before destruction, a haughty spirit before a fall" (Proverbs 16:18).

These ancient perspectives on the self and ego provide a valuable counterpoint to our modern conceptions. They remind us that the idea of a strong, independent self is not a universal or timeless concept but has evolved and varies across cultures.

3. The Renaissance and the Birth of Humanism

The Renaissance, typically from the 14th to the 17th century, marked a significant shift in Western thinking about the individual. This period saw a revival of interest in classical learning and a new emphasis on human potential and achievement.

Renaissance humanism, a philosophical and cultural movement that emerged during this time, placed a new emphasis on the dignity and worth of the individual. In his "Oration on the Dignity of Man," thinkers like Giovanni Pico Della Mirandola argued for humans' unique position in the cosmos as capable of deciding their nature through free will.

This period also saw the rise of the "Renaissance Man" ideal—an individual who could excel in multiple fields of study and artistic endeavours. Figures like Leonardo da Vinci embodied this ideal, showing the vast potential of human creativity and intellect.

We see a new focus on individual expression and the artist's unique vision in the arts. The rise of autobiography as a literary genre and the increasing prevalence of self-portraits in visual art reflects this growing interest in individual identity and self-expression.

While these developments celebrated human potential positively, they also laid the groundwork for a more ego-centric worldview. While the emphasis on individual achievement and self-expression was liberating in many respects, it also had the potential to fuel pride and self-aggrandisement.

4. The Enlightenment and the Cult of Reason

The Enlightenment, often called the "Age of Reason," further developed many humanistic ideas that emerged during the Renaissance. This 18th-century intellectual movement strongly emphasised rationality, individual rights, and scepticism towards traditional authorities.

Philosophers like John Locke argued for the importance of individual rights and the social contract, ideas that influenced political thinking and the formation of modern democracies. The "pursuit of happiness" as an individual right, enshrined in the United States Declaration of Independence, reflects this Enlightenment emphasis on personal fulfilment.

René Descartes' famous declaration "I, think, therefore I am" (Cogito, ergo sum) placed individual consciousness at the centre of philosophy. This radical doubt, which considered thinking of self as only certainty, had profound implications for how we conceive of the individual in relation to the world.

The Enlightenment also saw a decline in the authority of religious institutions and traditional hierarchies. While this led to many positive developments regarding individual freedom and scientific progress, it also removed some traditional checks on ego and self-interest.

The emphasis on reason and scepticism, while valuable in many ways, also had the potential to fuel arrogance. The idea that human reason could solve all problems and uncover all truths led to intellectual hubris that we still grapple with today.

5. The Industrial Revolution and the Rise of Individualism

The Industrial Revolution, which began in the late 18th century and continued through the 19th century, brought about dramatic changes in economic and social structures that further shaped our modern concept of self.

The shift from rural and craft-based economies to industrial production led to urbanisation and the breakdown of traditional community structures. In the new industrial cities, individuals were often cut off from extended family support networks and small-town life, leading to a greater emphasis on self-reliance.

The rise of wage labour and the opportunity for social mobility (however limited in reality) fostered a belief in individual agency and the ability to shape one's destiny. The "self-made man" became a cultural ideal embodied in stories of individuals rising from poverty to wealth through hard work and determination.

This period also saw the emergence of consumer culture, with mass-produced goods becoming increasingly available. The ability to express one's identity and status through consumer choices added a new dimension to individual self-expression.

However, these developments also had their dark side. The emphasis on individual success often came at the expense of community and social responsibility. The harsh realities of industrial capitalism led to exploitation and inequality, even as it promised individual opportunity.

6. Freud and the Unconscious Self

At the turn of the 20th century, new perspectives on the

human psyche profoundly influenced our understanding of the ego. Sigmund Freud's theories of the unconscious mind introduced a more complex and nuanced view of human psychology.

Freud's structural model of the psyche, which divided the mind into the id, ego, and superego, suggested that much of our behaviour is driven by unconscious forces beyond our conscious control. This challenged the Enlightenment notion of humans as purely rational beings and introduced a new element of internal conflict into our understanding of the self.

The concept of the ego in Freudian psychology - as the mediator between the id's instinctual desires and the superego's moral constraints - provided a new framework for understanding human behaviour and motivation. This more complex view of the self acknowledged the role of unconscious drives and internal conflicts in shaping our actions and self-perception.

While controversial and often challenged, Freud's ideas profoundly impacted Western culture. They introduced the idea that our conscious thoughts and actions might be driven by hidden motivations, adding complexity to individual identity.

7. The Impact of World Wars and Existentialism

The massive upheavals of the two World Wars in the first half of the 20th century profoundly impacted our ideas about the self and our place in the world. The scale of destruction and loss of life challenged many of the optimistic assumptions of the Enlightenment and Industrial Age.

In the aftermath of these conflicts, existentialist philosophy gained prominence. Thinkers like Jean-Paul Sartre emphasised individual freedom and responsibility in a world without inherent meaning. The existentialist slogan "existence precedes essence" suggested that individuals are solely responsible for creating meaning.

While existentialism emphasised individual freedom and responsibility, it also acknowledged the anxiety and uncertainty accompanying this freedom. Recognising life's inherent absurdity and the individual's responsibility to create meaning in the face of this absurdity added a new dimension to the self-concept.

This period also saw the rise of totalitarian regimes that sought to subsume individual identity into the collective. The horrors of these regimes led to a renewed emphasis on personal rights and freedoms in Western democracies, further cementing the importance of individualism in our culture.

8. The Post-War Economic Boom and Consumer Culture

The period following World War II, particularly in the United States and Western Europe, saw unprecedented economic growth and prosperity. This "Golden Age of Capitalism" had significant implications for individuals' views of themselves and their societal place.

The rise of suburban living, emphasising private space and nuclear family units, further reinforced the trend towards individualism. The ideal of the single-family home, complete with all the latest consumer goods, became a widely aspired-to symbol of success and self-sufficiency.

Advertising and marketing became increasingly sophisticated during this period, often appealing to individuals' desires for status and self-expression. The notion that one could construct and project an identity through consumer choices became increasingly prevalent.

This period also saw the rise of youth culture and the notion of the teenager as a distinct life stage. The idea that young people should "find themselves" and express their individuality became a cultural norm, further emphasising the importance of individual identity.

However, this emphasis on individual prosperity and self-expression often came at the expense of community engagement and social responsibility. Criticising this lifestyle as empty and materialistic would become a significant theme in the countercultural movements of the 1960s.

9. The Digital Revolution and the Networked Self

The advent of the internet and digital technologies in the late 20th and early 21st centuries have dramatically shifted how we conceive of and express individual identity since the Industrial Revolution.

Social media platforms have created new avenues for self-expression and self-promotion. The ability to curate and broadcast one's life and thoughts to a potentially global audience has led to what some scholars call the "networked self" - an identity constantly performed and negotiated in digital spaces.

The rise of personal branding, influencer culture, and the gig economy has further blurred the lines between personal and professional identity. For many, particularly younger generations, presenting oneself online has become crucial to social and economic life.

These technologies have also changed how we interact with information and form our worldviews. The ability to curate one's information environment through selective following and algorithmic recommendations can lead to echo chambers that reinforce existing beliefs and potentially fuel narcissism and self-aggrandisement.

At the same time, the internet has also created new forms of community and collective action. Online activism and crowdfunding platforms demonstrate the potential for digital technologies to foster cooperation and shared purpose.

The impact of these technologies on our conception of self is still unfolding, and their long-term effects on individual and collective psychology remain to be seen.

10. The Neuroscientific View of Self

Advances in neuroscience over the past few decades have offered new insights into the biological basis of consciousness and self-awareness. These findings have important implications for understanding the ego's and individual identity's nature.

Neuroscientific research suggests that our sense of self is a brain construct arising from the complex interplay of various neural processes. Studies of patients with brain injuries and neurological disorders have shown how damage to specific brain regions can profoundly alter one's sense of self.

The discovery of neuroplasticity - the brain's ability to change and adapt throughout life - has challenged notions of a fixed, unchanging self. This research suggests that our identities are more fluid and adaptable than previously thought.

Studies of meditation and mindfulness practices have shown that mental training can alter one's relationship to thoughts and sense of self. This aligns interestingly with ancient Buddhist concepts of no-self and the illusory nature of the ego.

While these findings provide fascinating insights into the nature of consciousness and identity, they also raise complex philosophical questions. If the self is a construct of the brain, what implications does this have for concepts like free will and moral responsibility?

11. The Self-Esteem Movement and Its Critics

The latter half of the 20th century saw the rise of the self-esteem movement, particularly in education and parenting philosophies. This movement, based on the idea that high self-esteem is crucial for success and well-being, has significantly affected how we think about individual worth and achievement.

Proponents of the self-esteem movement argued that boosting children's self-esteem would improve their academic performance, foster healthier relationships, and increase their success in life. This led to educational practices aimed at protecting children's self-esteem, such as avoiding negative feedback and providing praise regardless of achievement.

However, this movement has faced significant criticism in recent years. Critics argue that the focus on self-esteem has led to *a generation of individuals with an inflated sense of self-worth not matched by actual competence or achievement.* These disconnects, they suggest, can lead to **narcissism, entitlement, and an inability to handle criticism or failure**.

Research has shown that while healthy self-esteem is vital for well-being, it should be based on actual competence and achievement rather than empty praise. The concept of "growth mindset," which emphasises the ability to learn and improve through effort, has been proposed as a more productive alternative to simply boosting self-esteem.

This debate reflects broader tensions in our culture between promoting individual self-worth and maintaining achievement and social responsibility standards.

12. Individualism vs. Collectivism: A Global Perspective

While our focus has been primarily on the development of ego and individualism in Western culture, it is essential to recognise that this trajectory is not universal. Many cultures worldwide support a more collectivist orientation, prioritising group harmony and social roles over individual self-expression.

In many East Asian cultures, for instance, the concept of self is more fluid and contextual, defined by one's relationships and social roles. The Japanese concept of "amae," which refers to the desire to depend on others' benevolence, reflects a quite different understanding of the individual's relationship to society than the Western ideal of self-reliance.

Indigenous cultures often have a more holistic view of the self, seeing individuals as inseparable from their community and natural environment. This perspective challenges the Western notion of a bounded, autonomous self.

As globalisation brings diverse cultural perspectives into contact, we see complex interactions between individualist and collectivist value systems. In many non-Western countries, young people increasingly adopt individualistic attitudes, often influenced by Western media and consumer culture.

Understanding these cultural differences is crucial for developing a more nuanced view of ego and its societal role. It reminds us that our current "Woke in the Age of Ego" is not an inevitable stage of human development but a particular cultural configuration with its own strengths and weaknesses.

13. The Dark Side of Ego: Narcissism and Its Consequences

While a healthy sense of self is essential for psychological well-being, an inflated ego can lead to narcissism - an excessive need for admiration and a grandiose sense of self-importance. In recent years, some psychologists and social critics have argued that we are seeing a rise in narcissistic traits in Western societies, particularly among younger generations.

Narcissism, at its core, involves a deep-seated insecurity masked by an outward display of superiority. Narcissistic individuals often have difficulty keeping healthy relationships, as they struggle with empathy and tend to exploit others for their own gain.

The rise of social media has provided new outlets for narcissistic behaviour, allowing individuals to curate idealised versions of themselves for public consumption. The constant quest for likes, shares, and followers can feed into narcissistic tendencies.

At a societal level, narcissism can have profound consequences. Leaders with narcissistic traits may make decisions based on personal glory rather than the common good. In business, narcissistic CEOs might take excessive risks or engage in unethical behaviour to maintain their self-image of success.

The environmental crisis we currently face is partly a consequence of collective narcissism - a species-wide failure to consider the long-term consequences of our actions on the planet and future generations.

Addressing these issues requires balancing healthy self-esteem with an awareness of our interconnectedness and responsibilities to others and the world around us.

14. Technology and the Amplification of Ego

The rapid advancement of technology in recent decades

has provided unprecedented tools for self-expression and self-promotion, often amplifying egoistic tendencies in the process.

Social media platforms have created an environment where cultivating and projecting a carefully curated self-image has become normalised. The constant stream of likes, comments, and shares provides immediate feedback and validation, potentially reinforcing narcissistic behaviours.

The rise of the "quantified self" movement, where individuals track various aspects of their lives using technology, reflects a new level of self-focus. While this can lead to positive outcomes in terms of health and productivity, it also risks turning the self into a project of constant optimisation and comparison.

Virtual and augmented reality technologies offer new possibilities for ego expression and expansion. These technologies allow users to create and inhabit idealised versions of themselves, potentially blurring the lines between real and virtual identities.

Artificial Intelligence and machine learning algorithms, often designed to cater to individual preferences, can create personalised echo chambers reinforcing existing beliefs and biases. This algorithmic curation of reality can lead to an inflated sense of the importance of one's perspective.

The gig economy and digital entrepreneurship have created new avenues for individual achievement and self-branding. While this offers exciting opportunities, it also places increased pressure on individuals to market themselves and their skills constantly.

However, it is essential to note that technology also offers potential antidotes to excessive ego. Global connectivity can expose individuals to diverse perspectives, potentially fostering empathy and a more expansive worldview. Collaborative digital platforms show the power of collective action and shared knowledge.

As we navigate this digital landscape, the challenge is to harness technology's potential to enhance human connection and understanding rather than simply amplifying individual egos.

15. The Role of Education in Shaping the Self

Education plays a crucial role in shaping how individuals perceive themselves and their place in the world. Educational systems' structure and content reflect and reinforce societal values about individualism and collectivism.

In many Western education systems, there is a strong emphasis on individual achievement and competition. Standardised testing, individual grades, and personal accolades can foster a sense of individual exceptionalism. While this can motivate high achievement, it may also contribute to an inflated sense of self-importance.

While the recent focus on STEM (Science, Technology, Engineering, and Mathematics) education has been valuable in many ways, it has sometimes come at the expense of the humanities and social sciences. This shift could lead to a more technocratic worldview that neglects essential aspects of human experience and social dynamics.

However, there are also countervailing trends in education. The growing emphasis on social-emotional learning recognises the importance of empathy, cooperation, and self-awareness. Project-based learning and group work can help students understand the value of collaboration and diverse perspectives.

Some alternative educational philosophies, such as Montessori or Waldorf methods, emphasise holistic development and connection to community and nature. These approaches may offer valuable insights for balancing individual development with social responsibility.

Higher education, particularly in the humanities and social sciences, often challenges students to critically examine their assumptions and place themselves in broader historical and cultural contexts. This can play a crucial role in developing a more nuanced understanding of the self and its relation to society.

As we consider the role of education in the Woke in the Age of Ego, key questions emerge: How can we foster healthy self-esteem and individual potential while cultivating empathy, social responsibility, and an understanding of our interdependence? How can education prepare individuals for a rapidly changing world while grounding them in enduring human values?

16. The Media Landscape and the Cult of Personality

The evolution of media has significantly shaped our understanding of self and amplified certain egoistic tendencies. The rise of mass media in the 20th century, followed by the fragmentation and personalisation of Media in the digital age, has profoundly influenced how individuals perceive themselves and others.

The cult of celebrity, which began with the film industry and expanded through television and now social media, has created a culture of admiration for individual personalities. This has shaped aspirations and notions of success, often emphasising fame and visibility over other forms of achievement.

Reality TV, which gained popularity in the late 20th and early 21st centuries, normalised the idea that ordinary individuals could and should seek fame. This "democratisation" of celebrity has contributed to a culture where self-promotion and visibility are increasingly seen as virtues.

The 24-hour news cycle and personalisation of news consumption have also contributed to an increasingly ego-centric worldview. The ability to curate one's news sources can lead to confirmation bias and a narrowing of perspective, potentially inflating the perceived importance of one's views.

Social media influencers represent a new category of celebrity, often built on cultivating and monetising a personal brand. While this opens up new opportunities for individual expression and entrepreneurship, it also reinforces the idea that the self is a product to be packaged and sold.

However, media also has the potential to broaden perspectives and foster empathy. Documentaries, long-form journalism, and diverse storytelling can expose individuals to different lives and experiences, potentially counteracting narrow egocentrism.

As media continues to evolve, the challenge lies in fostering literacy and critical thinking skills that allow individuals to navigate this complex landscape without losing sight of broader social realities and responsibilities.

17. The Economic Landscape and Its Impact on Ego

The economic systems within which we operate profoundly impact how we perceive ourselves and our place in society. The rise of neoliberal capitalism in the late 20th century has significantly shaped our current "Woke in the Age of Ego."

The emphasis on free markets and individual economic

agency has reinforced the idea of the self as a competitive, self-interested actor. The notion of "human capital" - the idea that individuals should continuously invest in and market their skills and attributes - has turned the self into an ongoing economic project.

The gig economy and the rise of entrepreneurship culture have further individualised economic activity. While these trends offer new opportunities for flexibility and self-direction, they also place increased pressure on individuals to constantly sell themselves and their skills. This can lead to a conflation of personal identity with economic value, potentially exacerbating narcissistic tendencies.

Income inequality, which has grown in many countries in recent decades, can fuel grandiosity among the wealthy and feelings of inadequacy among those struggling economically. The visibility of extreme wealth, mainly through media and social media, can skew perceptions of what constitutes "normal" or "successful" living standards.

Consumer culture, a key feature of modern capitalism, plays a significant role in shaping ego and identity. The idea that we can express and enhance our identities through purchasing decisions has become deeply ingrained. This constant invitation to self-definition through consumption can feed into narcissistic tendencies and a never-ending quest for self-improvement through acquisition.

However, there are also countervailing economic trends that challenge this individualistic paradigm. The growth of the sharing economy, while not without its problems, suggests a shift towards more collaborative economic models. Increased awareness of environmental issues has led to a growing critique of consumerism and a search for more sustainable economic approaches.

The concept of "stakeholder capitalism," which considers the interests of all parties affected by a company's actions, not just shareholders, represents an attempt to broaden the focus beyond individual or corporate self-interest. Similarly, the B Corp movement, certifying companies that meet specific social and environmental performance standards, accountability, and transparency, reflects a growing recognition of business's broader responsibilities.

As we navigate the complex relationship between economics and ego, key questions emerge: How can we create economic systems that foster individual initiative and innovation without exacerbating narcissism and social division? How can we balance the drive for personal financial security with a sense of social responsibility and interconnectedness?

18. The Environmental Crisis and the Challenges to Ego

The growing awareness of environmental issues, particularly climate change, poses a significant challenge to ego-centric worldviews. The reality of global ecological interdependence forces us to confront the limitations of individualistic thinking and the consequences of collective human activity.

The environmental crisis can be seen partly as a result of excessive ego—a collective failure to consider the long-term impacts of our actions on the planet and future generations. Prioritising short-term individual or national interests over long-term global sustainability reflects a kind of species-level narcissism.

However, the environmental movement also offers potential antidotes to excessive ego. Recognising our dependence on and connection to natural systems can foster a more humble and holistic sense of self. Environmental education often emphasises systems thinking and interconnectedness, which can counteract narrowly individualistic perspectives.

Philosophers and ecologists developed the concept of the "ecological self," which suggests expanding self-identity to include the natural world. This perspective sees human identity as inextricably linked with the broader web of life, challenging the notion of a separate, autonomous ego.

Indigenous perspectives on the relationship between humans and nature, which often emphasise harmony and stewardship rather than dominance, offer valuable alternatives to ego-centric views of the environment. As these perspectives gain more attention in environmental discourse, they challenge dominant Western notions of self and nature.

The need for collective action to address environmental challenges also pushes against individualistic tendencies. The reality that no individual or nation can solve climate change alone necessitates cooperation and a recognition of our shared fate as a species.

However, environmental issues can also trigger ego-defensive reactions. Climate change denial, for instance, can be seen in part as a defence mechanism against threats to one's worldview or lifestyle. The enormity of environmental challenges can also lead to a retreat into individual concerns, as global issues seem too overwhelming to confront.

As we grapple with environmental challenges, we must reconsider our place in the world and our responsibilities to the planet and future generations. This reconsideration can foster a more expansive and humble sense of self, one that recognises our interdependence with the natural world and each other.

19. Spirituality and Religion in the Woke in the Age of Ego

Spirituality and religion play complex and multifaceted roles in shaping concepts of self and ego. While many religious and spiritual traditions emphasise humility and transcendence of the ego, how these traditions are practised and interpreted in modern contexts can sometimes reinforce ego-centric tendencies.

Traditional religious teachings often emphasise the importance of transcending the individual self to connect with something more significant, whether conceived as God, the universe, or the broader human community. Practices like prayer, meditation, and service to others often aim to diminish the ego's control and foster a sense of interconnectedness.

However, the individualisation of spirituality in many Western contexts has led to what some scholars call "self-spirituality" - a focus on personal growth and self-realisation that can sometimes reinforce rather than transcend ego. The popularisation of concepts like "manifesting" and "the law of attraction" can sometimes veer into magical thinking about the power of individual will.

The prosperity gospel movement, which links faith with material success, is a stark example of how religious ideas can be adapted to reinforce ego and materialism. This theology, which suggests that God wants believers to be wealthy, can provide divine justification for self-interest and accumulation.

Conversely, many contemporary spiritual movements draw on Eastern and Western traditions to offer practices for ego transcendence. Mindfulness and meditation, which have gained widespread popularity, are often framed as ways to observe and ultimately detach from the ego's constant narratives.

The growth of interest in psychedelic spirituality, while controversial, reflects a desire for ego-dissolving experiences that provide a broader perspective on the self and its place in the world. This interest harkens back to using entheogens in many traditional spiritual practices.

Interfaith dialogue and the growing recognition of religious pluralism can challenge ego-centric worldviews by exposing individuals to diverse perspectives on the nature of self and reality. Recognising that one's religious or spiritual beliefs are not universal can foster humility and openness.

As we navigate the complex landscape of spirituality and religion in The Woke in the Age of Ego, key questions emerge: How can spiritual and religious practices be engaged in ways that genuinely transcend rather than reinforce ego? How can we balance the search for personal meaning and growth with recognising our interconnectedness and responsibilities to others?

20. Philosophy and the Questioning of Self

Throughout history, philosophy has grappled with questions of self, identity, and the nature of ego. In our current Woke in the Age of Ego, revisiting and engaging with these philosophical inquiries can provide valuable perspectives and tools for critically examining our assumptions about the self.

Ancient Greek philosophy, emphasising self-examination (exemplified by Socrates' dictum, "Know thyself"), provides a foundation for questioning our understanding of self. The Stoic philosophers, in particular, emphasised distinguishing between what is within our control (thoughts and actions) and what is not. This offers an antidote to the illusion of total individual agency that often fuels the ego.

Eastern philosophical traditions offer different perspectives on the nature of self. Buddhist philosophy challenges the notion of a fixed, unchanging ego with its concept of "anatta" or "no-self." The Taoist concept of "wu wei" or "non-doing" suggests acting in harmony with the natural flow of things rather than asserting individual will against the world.

In Western philosophy, thinkers like David Hume questioned the existence of a unified, persistent self, arguing instead that the self is a bundle of perceptions. This view challenges the notion of a stable ego and aligns interestingly with some contemporary neuroscientific perspectives.

Existentialist philosophers like Jean-Paul Sartre emphasised individual freedom and responsibility but also acknowledged the anxiety that comes with this freedom. The existentialist recognition of life's inherent absurdity can serve as a check on ego inflation, reminding us of the ultimate limitations of individual significance.

Postmodern philosophy, with its scepticism toward grand narratives and fixed identities, offers tools for deconstructing ego-centric worldviews. Thinkers like Jacques Derrida and Michel Foucault encourage us to examine how language, power structures, and cultural narratives shape our sense of self.

Feminist philosophy has significantly contributed to our understanding of self and identity. It highlights how gender shapes our experiences and challenges androcentric assumptions in traditional philosophical accounts of the self.

More recently, philosophy of mind and cognitive science have raised new questions about the nature of consciousness and self-awareness. Debates about free will and the extent to which factors outside our conscious control determine our thoughts and actions challenge simplistic notions of individual agency.

Environmental philosophy and ethics have expanded our consideration of self, including our relationship with the natural world. Philosophers like Arne Naess developed the concept of the "ecological self," which suggests a radical expansion of self-identity beyond the boundaries of the individual ego.

Engaging with these diverse philosophical perspectives can provide valuable tools for critically examining our assumptions about self and ego. Philosophy encourages us to question our beliefs and consider alternative viewpoints, potentially fostering a more nuanced and humble understanding of our place in the world.

21. The Role of Art in Reflecting and Shaping Ego

Art has always been crucial in exploring, expressing, and shaping concepts of self and ego. As both a mirror and a moulder of culture, art offers unique insights into how we perceive ourselves and our place in the world.

The Renaissance saw the artist's rise as an individual creator, reflected in the increasing prevalence of artist signatures and self-portraits. This shift marked a new emphasis on individual genius and self-expression that has profoundly influenced Western art ever since.

The Romantic movement in the late 18th and early 19th centuries further emphasised individual emotional expression and the cult of genius. This period saw the emergence of the artist as a semi-mythical figure, separate from and often at odds with mainstream society.

The advent of photography in the 19th century democratised self-representation, allowing individuals to craft and disseminate images of themselves in unprecedented ways. This trend has exponentially increased with the rise of digital photography and social media, turning self-representation into a daily practice for many.

Modern and postmodern art movements have often engaged

critically with notions of self and identity. Surrealism explored the unconscious mind, challenging rational, ego-driven understandings of self. Pop Art examined the relationship between individual identity and mass culture. Performance art has often involved radical explorations of the body and identity.

Contemporary art frequently grapples with identity politics, exploring how race, gender, sexuality, and cultural background shape our sense of self. Artists like Cindy Sherman, who photographs herself in various guises, directly confront identity construction and representation issues.

Digital and new media art forms offer new possibilities for exploring fluid and multiple identities. Virtual reality art, for instance, allows for immersive experiences that can challenge fixed notions of self.

However, the art world itself is not immune to ego-centric tendencies. The cult of the artist as a singular genius, the commodification of art in the global market, and the spectacle of celebrity artists all reflect and potentially reinforce ego-driven aspects of our culture.

At the same time, many contemporary artists are using their platforms to challenge ego-centric worldviews. Socially engaged art practices often emphasise collaboration and community involvement over individual expression. Environmental artists are creating works that highlight our interconnectedness with nature.

As we consider the role of art in the Woke in the Age of Ego, key questions emerge: How can art continue to provide critical perspectives on our understanding of self and identity? How can artistic practices foster connection and empathy in an increasingly individualistic world?

22. The Digital Self: Identity in the Virtual Age

The rise of digital technology has profoundly affected how we construct, present, and understand our identities. In our hyper-connected world, the "digital self" concept has become increasingly relevant.

Social media platforms offer unprecedented opportunities for self-presentation and identity curation. Users can carefully craft online personas, highlighting certain aspects of their lives and personalities while downplaying others. This ability to control one's image can be empowering, but it also raises questions about authenticity and the potential disconnect between online and offline selves.

The phenomenon of "digital dualism" - the belief that the online and offline worlds are separate and distinct - is increasingly being challenged. Instead, many scholars argue for a view of "augmented reality," where digital and physical experiences are interwoven and mutually influential. This perspective suggests that our digital activities are not separate from our "real" selves but integral to our identity.

Online anonymity and the use of avatars in virtual worlds allow for experimentation with different identities. This fluidity can be liberating, allowing individuals to explore aspects of themselves that they might be unable to express physically. However, it also raises questions about the stability and coherence of identity.

The concept of "context collapse" in social media, where multiple audiences (friends, family, colleagues, etc.) are flattened into a single context, creates new challenges for identity management. Users must navigate how to present themselves authentically while being mindful of diverse audience expectations.

Digital footprints and data trails create a kind of passive digital identity that exists beyond our conscious self-presentation. The information collected about our online behaviours, preferences, and interactions forms a data double that can be used to predict our future behaviours or make decisions about us.

The rise of AI and machine learning adds another layer to digital identity. Predictive algorithms and personalisation technologies shape our online experiences based on our past behaviours, potentially reinforcing certain aspects of our identity while limiting exposure to others.

As we navigate this digital landscape, key questions emerge: How do we maintain a sense of authentic self across multiple digital platforms? How do we balance the benefits of digital self-expression with the need for privacy and data protection? How do we ensure that our digital selves contribute to, rather than detract, our overall well-being and social connections?

23. The Neuroscience of Ego: Insights from Brain Research

Advances in neuroscience have offered new insights into the neural basis of self and ego, offering a biological perspective on these psychological and philosophical concepts.

Research suggests that the brain does not have a single "self-center." Instead, our sense of self emerges from the complex interplay of multiple brain regions and processes. This aligns with philosophical perspectives that question the existence of a unitary, essential self.

Studies of the Default Mode Network (DMN), a set of interconnected brain regions active when we are not focused on the external world, have been particularly illuminating. The DMN is associated with self-referential thinking, autobiographical memory, and envisioning the future.

Overactivity in this network has been linked to rumination and depression, suggesting a potential neurological basis for excessive self-focus.

Neuroscientific research on meditation has shown that practices aimed at transcending the ego can lead to measurable changes in brain activity and structure. Long-term meditators show reduced activity in the DMN and increased connectivity between brain regions associated with self-regulation and cognitive control.

Studies of psychiatric conditions that involve disturbances of the self, such as schizophrenia and depersonalisation disorder, provide insights into the neural underpinnings of our sense of self. These conditions often include disruptions in brain networks involved in self-processing and bodily awareness.

Research on mirror neurons, which activate when an individual performs an action and when they observe someone else performing the same action, has shed light on the neural basis of empathy and social cognition. This research suggests that our brains are wired for social connection and understanding others, challenging strictly ego-centric views of cognition.

Neuroscientific perspectives on free will and decision-making have essential implications for understanding individual agency and responsibility. Research suggests that many of our decisions are started unconsciously before we are aware of making a choice, challenging simplistic notions of conscious control and self-determination.

As we integrate neuroscientific insights into our understanding of self and ego, it is crucial to avoid reductionist interpretations. While brain research provides valuable information about the neural correlates of self-experience, it still needs to negate the importance of psychological, social, and cultural factors in shaping our sense of self.

24. Ego and Leadership: Implications for Governance and Organization

The role of ego in leadership has significant implications for how organisations and societies are governed. Understanding the interplay between ego, power, and leadership is crucial in our current Woke in the Age of Ego.

Healthy self-esteem and confidence are often seen as necessary traits for effective leadership. However, when these traits become narcissistic or excessive, they can lead to detrimental outcomes. Leaders with inflated egos may become resistant to feedback, overlook vital information that differs from their views, or prioritise personal glory over organisational or societal needs.

Robert K. Greenleaf's "servant leadership "concept offers a counterpoint to ego-driven leadership models. This approach emphasises the leader's role in serving others and the greater good rather than self-aggrandisement.

Research in organisational psychology has explored the impact of leader narcissism on team performance and organisational culture. While narcissistic leaders can sometimes drive short-term results through their charisma and vision, they often create toxic work environments and long-term instability.

In the political sphere, the rise of populist leaders in various parts of the world has been linked to appeals to collective narcissism - a belief in the greatness and victimisation of one's group. This phenomenon shows how individual and collective forms of ego can interact in powerful and sometimes dangerous ways.

Scholars like Edgar Schein advocate for "humble leadership," which suggests that effective modern leaders must move beyond the heroic, ego-driven model. In complex, rapidly changing environments, leaders need humility to acknowledge what they do not know and learn from those around them.

Recent corporate scandals and failures have highlighted the dangers of unchecked ego in business leadership. This has led to increased emphasis on ethical leadership and corporate governance structures that can provide checks on executive power.

In international relations, ego-driven leadership can worsen conflicts and hinder diplomatic solutions. Conversely, leaders who transcend narrow ego-centric or nationalistic perspectives are often more effective at building coalitions and solving global challenges.

As we consider the future of leadership in the Woke in the Age of Ego, key questions emerge: How can we select and develop leaders confident in their ability to act decisively but humble enough to consider diverse perspectives? How can organisational and political systems be designed to harness the positive aspects of ego while mitigating its potential adverse effects?

25. Ego and Creativity: The Double-Edged Sword

The relationship between ego and creativity is complex and often paradoxical. While a certain degree of self-belief and individualism can fuel creative expression, excessive ego can stifle creativity and innovation.

Many outstanding artistic and scientific achievements have been driven by individuals with strong egos and a belief in their unique vision. The willingness to challenge conventional wisdom and persist in the face of criticism—often fuelled by a strong sense of self—has been crucial to many creative breakthroughs.

However, an inflated ego can also lead to creative stagnation. When individuals become too attached to their ideas or too confident in their abilities, they may become less open to new influences, constructive criticism, or collaborative opportunities.

The concept of "flow," developed by psychologist Mihaly Csikszentmihalyi, describes an optimal creative experience in which self-consciousness disappears, and individuals become fully immersed in their task. This suggests that some of our most creative moments involve transcending ego.

In the business world, there's growing recognition of the importance of "creative abrasion" - the productive friction that occurs when diverse perspectives and ideas collide. This process often requires individuals to set aside their egos and engage openly with challenging viewpoints.

The rise of design thinking and other collaborative creative methodologies emphasises the importance of empathy, user-focused thinking, and iterative processes. These approaches often require creators to suspend their egos and preconceptions to understand and genuinely address the needs of others.

Studies in cognitive psychology have shown that specific ego-transcending experiences, such as awe in nature or meditation, can enhance creativity by breaking habitual thought patterns and fostering more flexible thinking.

The increasing emphasis on interdisciplinary approaches in arts and sciences recognises that major innovations often occur at the intersection of different fields. This requires individuals to move beyond the ego-driven desire to be the sole expert and instead embrace collaborative, boundary-crossing work.

As we navigate the relationship between ego and creativity in the modern world, key questions emerge: How can we foster the self-confidence necessary for creative risk-taking while cultivating the humility needed for continuous learning and collaboration? How can educational and organisational systems nurture creativity without excessively inflating individual egos?

26. Ego, Consumption, and Sustainability

The relationship between ego, consumption patterns, and environmental sustainability is critical in our current Woke in the Age of Ego. How we construct and express our identities through consumption has significant implications for the health of our planet.

Consumer culture often feeds on and reinforces ego by suggesting that identity and status can be acquired through purchases. The constant cycle of new products and planned obsolescence stimulates continuous consumption and strengthens a sense of belonging to material possessions.

The rise of "conspicuous consumption," coined by economist Thorstein Veblen, refers to buying luxury goods to display economic power and status. This ego-driven consumption often comes at a high environmental cost.

Fast fashion, which relies on rapidly changing trends and low-cost production, is a prime example of how ego-driven consumption patterns can lead to significant environmental degradation—the desire to constantly update one's image through clothing results in massive waste and resource depletion.

Social media has amplified these trends by providing new platforms for displaying consumption and lifestyle. The pressure to present a curated, enviable life online can drive increased consumption and waste.

However, countervailing trends also challenge ego-driven consumption. The minimalist movement, for instance, advocates reducing possessions and focusing on experiences rather than material goods. This approach often involves a critique of ego-driven consumption and a search for more sustainable ways of living.

Despite commercialisation, the "sharing economy "concept reflects a potential shift from individual ownership to more collaborative consumption models. This trend suggests constructing identities based on access and experience rather than possession.

The growing awareness of environmental issues has led to the rise of "ethical consumption" and "conscious consumerism." While these movements still operate within a consumerist framework, they reflect an attempt to align purchasing decisions with broader values and concerns beyond individual ego gratification.

Some environmental philosophers and activists advocate a more radical shift away from consumption-based identities. They advocate finding sources of meaning and self-worth unrelated to material possessions or economic status.

As we grapple with the urgent need for environmental sustainability, key questions emerge: How can we construct and express identities without relying on unsustainable consumption? How can we shift cultural values away from ego-driven materialism toward more collective and ecological understandings of self?

27. Ego and Well-being: Psychological Perspectives

The relationship between ego and psychological well-being is complex and often paradoxical. While a healthy sense of self is crucial for mental health, excessive ego-centrism can lead to various psychological issues.

Positive psychology research suggests that a certain level of self-esteem and self-efficacy is essential for well-being. Individuals who believe in their ability to face challenges and achieve goals tend to have better mental health outcomes.

However, studies have also shown links between excessive self-focus and various psychological problems. Narcissism, at its extreme, is classified as a personality disorder characterised by a grandiose sense of self-importance, a need for admiration, and a lack of empathy.

Research on social media use has found complex relationships with well-being. While these platforms can provide avenues for self-expression and connection, excessive use and social comparison can lead to increased anxiety, depression, and feelings of loneliness.

The "quiet ego" concept, developed by psychologists Heidi Wayment and Jack Bauer, suggests that well-being is enhanced when individuals balance self-interest with concern for others and the broader world. This involves cultivating humility, compassion, and a sense of connectedness.

Mindfulness and meditation practices, which often involve observing thoughts and emotions without identifying with them, have been shown to have numerous psychological benefits. These practices can help individuals develop a more flexible, less ego-driven relationship with their experiences.

Psychological research on prosocial behaviour suggests that

serving others can significantly boost well-being. This challenges purely ego-centric models of happiness and indicates the importance of transcending narrow self-interest.

Ecopsychology explores the relationship between human well-being and connection with the natural world. This perspective suggests that excessive ego-centrism harms the environment and cuts us off from a vital source of psychological health.

Terror Management Theory, developed by social psychologists, suggests that much of human behaviour is driven by the ego's attempt to manage the existential anxiety that comes from awareness of our mortality. This theory has implications for understanding various social and individual behaviours in the Woke in the Age of Ego.

As we consider the relationship between ego and well-being, key questions emerge: How can we foster a sense of self that is strong enough to provide resilience and agency but flexible enough to adapt to life's challenges? How can psychological interventions and social structures support a healthier balance between individual ego needs and broader relational and ecological well-being?

28. Conclusion: Navigating and Transcending the Woke in the Age of Ego

As we conclude our exploration of the foundations of ego in modern society, it's clear that we are navigating complex and often contradictory currents. The emphasis on individual identity and self-expression that characterises our age has brought many benefits - personal freedoms, creative innovations, and the recognition of diverse identities and experiences. Yet, it has also fostered narcissism, social atomisation, and a sometimes myopic focus on self-interest at the expense of collective well-being.

The challenges we face in the 21st century—from climate change to growing inequality to the ethical quandaries posed by emerging technologies—require us to find a balance between individual agency and collective responsibility. Strong individuals can bring creativity and initiative. Still, we also need empathy, cooperation, and long-term thinking to recognise our fundamental interconnectedness.

As we move forward, we might consider how we can foster what some philosophers have called an "ethical ego" - a sense of self that is strong enough to act with conviction and creativity but also humble enough to recognise its limitations and responsibilities to others. This might involve:

1. Cultivating critical self-reflection means regularly **examining** our assumptions, biases, and the **sources** of our beliefs about ourselves and the world.

2. Practicing empathy and perspective-taking: **Actively seeking** to understand viewpoints different from ours.

3. Engaging with diverse philosophical and spiritual traditions: Drawing **insights** from various cultures and periods about the nature of self and our place in the world.

4. Balancing self-care with care for others: We must recognise that our well-being is **inextricably linked to** the well-being of **others** and our environment.

5. Embracing complexity and uncertainty: **Moving beyond simplistic, ego-affirming narratives** to grapple with the nuances and ambiguities of real-world issues.

6. Fostering connection: Building **genuine** relationships and community ties beyond digital networks.

7. Engaging in practices that transcend ego: Whether through art, meditation, nature experiences, or other means, regularly

stepping outside our habitual self-narratives.

8. Contributing to something larger than ourselves: Finding ways to **align our efforts** with broader social and environmental goals.

As we navigate the Woke in the Age of Ego, we are called upon to write a new chapter in the long human story of self-understanding. Drawing on the wisdom of the past, the insights of the present, and our hopes for the future, we can strive to create a more balanced, compassionate, and sustainable relationship between self and the world.

In doing so, we may find that the most fulfilling expression of individuality comes not from inflating the ego but from recognising our place in the vast, interconnected web of life - unique, yes, but also fundamentally a part of something far more significant than ourselves.

In our extensive exploration of the ego in modern society, it's clear that we are at a critical juncture. The Woke in the Age of Ego, which emphasises individual identity, self-expression, and personal achievement, has brought remarkable advancements and significant challenges. As we look to the future, the question becomes not how to eliminate the ego—which is neither possible nor desirable—but how to transcend its limitations and harness its potential in service of individual fulfilment and collective flourishing.

This transcendence might involve several key shifts:

1. From separation to interconnection: We recognise that we are inextricably linked with others and the natural world. This does not negate individuality but contextualises it within a broader web of relationships and responsibilities.

2. From scarcity to abundance mindset: Moving beyond the

ego's tendency to work from a place of lack and competition towards a recognition of the fundamental abundance of human creativity and natural resources when adequately stewarded.

3. From short-term gratification to long-term vision: We must cultivate the ability to consider the longer-term consequences of our actions, both for ourselves and future generations.

4. From rigid to flexible identity: Developing a sense of self that is strong enough to provide stability but flexible enough to adapt to changing circumstances and incorporate new understandings.

5. From passive consumption to active creation: Shifting from defining ourselves primarily through what we consume to finding fulfilment in what we create and contribute.

6. From ego-centric to eco-centric thinking: Expanding our sphere of concern and identity to include the broader ecological systems that sustain us.

7. From either/or to both/and thinking: Moving beyond simplistic dichotomies to embrace the complexity and paradoxes inherent in human experience and the natural world.

These shifts require multiple individual, interpersonal, institutional, and cultural changes. They involve intellectual understanding, emotional intelligence, embodied practices, and new forms of social organisation.

Education will play a crucial role in this transformation. We need educational approaches that impart knowledge and skills and cultivate wisdom, empathy, and ecological awareness. This might involve integrating contemplative practices, systems thinking, and experiential learning into curricula at all levels.

Technology, which has amplified ego-centric tendencies in many ways, also has the potential to facilitate this transcendence. Virtual reality, for instance, could cultivate empathy by allowing people to experience life from vastly different perspectives. Social media platforms could be redesigned to encourage more profound, meaningful connections rather than superficial self-promotion.

We need systems in governance and economics that align individual incentives with collective well-being. This might involve new forms of participatory democracy, economic models that internalise social and environmental costs, and leadership paradigms that emphasise service and stewardship.

Art and culture are vital in helping us imagine and embody new ways of being. We need stories, images, and experiences that inspire us to see beyond the limitations of the ego and connect with something larger than ourselves.

Ultimately, transcending the Woke in the Age of Ego is not about denying or suppressing the self but expanding our understanding of what the self is and can be. It is about recognising that the most profound expressions of individuality often come not from inflating the ego but from connecting deeply with others and the world around us.

As we face unprecedented global challenges - from climate change to inequality to the ethical quandaries of emerging technologies - this expanded sense of self is desirable and necessary. Our future depends on our ability to act from a place of enlightened self-interest that recognises the fundamental interdependence of all life.

The journey beyond the Woke in the Age of Ego is not a destination but an ongoing process of individual and collective growth. It requires courage, creativity, and commitment. But in embarking on this journey, we open ourselves to new possibilities for fulfilment, connection, and meaning - possibilities that point toward a more sustainable, just, and vibrant future for all.

CHAPTER 2: POLITICS AND POWER

1. Introduction: The Ego in the Political Arena

Politics, at its core, is about the distribution and exercise of power within society. It is also, inevitably, a realm where human egos clash, compete, and sometimes cooperate. In this chapter, we will explore the intricate relationship between ego and political power, examining how personal and collective egos shape political landscapes, influence decision-making, and impact the very fabric of our societies.

The political arena often amplifies the dynamics of ego we see in other aspects of life. The stakes are high, the spotlight is bright, and the potential for glory and infamy is immense. This environment can bring out the best and worst aspects of human nature, making it a crucial study area in examining the Woke in the Age of Ego.

As we delve into this topic, we will consider historical examples, contemporary case studies, psychological insights, and philosophical perspectives. We will also draw parallels between modern political phenomena and warnings in biblical and other ancient texts, seeking timeless wisdom to guide us in navigating the complex intersection of ego and power in the 21st century.

2. The Psychology of Political Leadership

Political leadership requires self-confidence and assertiveness. Leaders must believe in their ability to guide and inspire others, make difficult decisions, and weather criticism and opposition. In this sense, a healthy ego is often a prerequisite for effective leadership.

However, the very traits that can make for strong leadership - confidence, charisma, decisiveness - can also, when taken to extremes, lead to destructive forms of ego-driven behaviour. Political psychologists have long studied the personality traits of leaders, identifying patterns that can lead to effective governance and catastrophic failures.

The concept of narcissistic leadership, developed by psychologist Michael Maccoby, suggests that many successful leaders display narcissistic traits such as grandiosity, a need for admiration, and a lack of empathy. While these traits can drive vision and change, they can also lead to reckless decision-making, an inability to accept criticism, and prioritising personal glory over the public good.

Historical examples abound of leaders whose outsized egos led to disastrous consequences. From Napoleon's ill-fated invasion of Russia to Hitler's megalomaniacal vision of a thousand-year Reich, history is abounding with cautionary tales of what can happen when political power amplifies and enables extreme ego.

Yet, it's important to note that not all strong leaders are driven by oversized egos. Robert K. Greenleaf introduced the concept of "servant leadership," which proposes a leadership model focused on the growth and well-being of communities and their people. Leaders like Nelson Mandela and Mahatma Gandhi exemplified this form of leadership, transcending personal ego to serve a more significant cause.

3. The Role of Ego in Political Ideologies

Political ideologies often express the collective ego, providing frameworks through which groups assert their identity, values, and vision for society. Whether left or right, liberal or conservative, political ideologies can become ego investments, shaping how individuals and groups see themselves and their place in the world.

The strength of these ego investments can lead to political polarisation, where adherents of different ideologies struggle to find common ground or even acknowledge the legitimacy of opposing viewpoints. This dynamic is exacerbated in the age of social media and personalised news feeds, where individuals can quickly surround themselves with like-minded voices, reinforcing their ideological ego investments.

Nationalism can be seen as collective narcissism, where the nation becomes an extension of the ego. While healthy patriotism can foster social cohesion and civic engagement, extreme nationalism can lead to xenophobia, conflict, and a dangerous disregard for global concerns like climate change.

On the other hand, political philosophies that emphasise collective welfare over individual or national self-interest—such as certain forms of socialism or global humanitarianism—can be seen as attempts to transcend ego-driven politics. However, even these ideologies can become ego investments if adherents become overly attached to their moral superiority or the infallibility of their worldview.

4. Ego and Political Discourse

The quality of political discourse is crucial to the health of any democracy. However, in recent years, many observers have noted a decline in the civility and substance of political debate, a trend often attributed to the rise of ego-driven politics.

Social media has provided new platforms for political

expression and amplified some of the more ego-driven aspects of political discourse. The quest for likes, retweets, and viral content can incentivise provocative and divisive statements over nuanced discussion. Politicians and pundits who can craft pithy, attention-grabbing messages often gain outsized influence, regardless of the depth or accuracy of their ideas.

The phenomenon of "virtue signalling"—where individuals make public statements primarily to enhance their image rather than effect real change—can be seen as an expression of ego in political discourse. While raising awareness of critical issues can be valuable, the performative nature of online activism risks prioritising personal brand-building over substantive action.

The ego-driven nature of much political discourse can make it challenging to find common ground or admit error. When political positions become tied to personal identity, changing one's mind or compromising can feel like a threat to the ego. This dynamic contributes to political gridlock and the inability to address complex, long-term challenges that require cooperation and flexibility.

5. Power, Corruption, and the Ego

The adage "power corrupts, and absolute power corrupts absolutely" speaks to the dangerous interplay between power and ego. Gaining political power can be a potent ego boost, potentially leading to an inflated sense of self-importance and capability.

Psychological studies have shown that power can change how people think and behave. It can increase confidence but decrease empathy, leading to more self-centred decision-making. This "power paradox," as psychologist Dacher Keltner describes it, suggests that the traits that help people gain power—empathy, collaboration, and fairness—are often eroded by the experience of having power.

Corruption in politics can often be traced to ego-driven desires for wealth, status, or legacy. Politicians prioritising personal gain over public service usually show that their ego has overtaken their sense of duty and responsibility.

However, it's important to note that power doesn't inevitably lead to corruption. Leaders who maintain a strong ethical framework, remain connected to the people they serve, and cultivate humility can use their power to effect positive change. The challenge is to create political systems and cultures that encourage this type of leadership while providing checks against the potential abuses of ego-driven power.

6. The Media, Politics, and Ego

The relationship between politics and media has always been complex, but it has taken on new dimensions in the wake of the Woke in the Age of Ego. The 24-hour news cycle and the proliferation of media outlets have created an environment in which politicians must constantly compete for attention.

This atmosphere can reward those most adept at self-promotion and attention-grabbing behaviour, often at the expense of substantive policy discussion. The rise of the politician as a celebrity, with personal charisma and media savvy sometimes outweighing experience or ability, is a hallmark of ego-driven politics in the media age.

The "fake news" phenomenon and the erosion of trust in traditional media sources can also be seen through the ego lens. When faced with information that challenges their worldview or self-image, individuals may dismiss it as false or biased rather than engage with it critically. This ego-protective behaviour, amplified by social media algorithms that create echo chambers, can lead to the fragmentation of shared reality, undermining democratic discourse.

On the other hand, media can also play a crucial role in holding ego-driven politicians accountable. Investigative journalism, fact-checking initiatives, and platforms for diverse voices can help to counterbalance the potential excesses of political egos.

7. Ego and International Relations

The interplay of national egos can have profound consequences in international relations. Diplomatic negotiations often involve balancing asserting national interests with finding mutually beneficial solutions.

Historical examples like the Treaty of Versailles after World War I prove how wounded national egos and desires for retribution can lead to agreements that sow the seeds of future conflicts. Conversely, initiatives like the Marshall Plan after World War II show how transcending narrow self-interest favouring mutual recovery and cooperation can yield long-term benefits for all parties.

In the current global landscape, ego-driven nationalism poses significant challenges to addressing transnational issues like climate change, pandemics, and economic inequality. When nations prioritise short-term self-interest over long-term global welfare, it becomes difficult to craft effective collective responses to shared threats.

The concept of "face" in international relations, fundamental in some cultures, shows how ego considerations can affect diplomacy. The need to avoid loss of face can sometimes prevent leaders from making necessary compromises or admitting mistakes, potentially escalating conflicts or preventing their resolution.

8. Grassroots Movements and the Transcendence of Ego

While much of our discussion has focused on the negative impacts of ego in politics, it's essential to recognise that political engagement can also be a powerful vehicle for transcending individual ego to serve a more significant cause.

Grassroots political movements often exemplify a form of collective action that incorporates individual egos into a larger purpose. From the civil rights movement to environmental activism, history gives numerous examples of individuals setting aside personal comfort and safety to fight for broader social change.

The concept of "solidarity," central to many progressive political movements, is a form of ego transcendence. Individuals can expand their sphere of concern beyond personal or national self-interest by recognising shared struggles and interconnected fates.

However, even grassroots movements are not immune to the pitfalls of ego. Leadership struggles, ideological purity tests, and the desire for personal recognition can sometimes undermine the effectiveness of these movements. The challenge is to channel the passion and commitment of individual egos toward collective goals without allowing those egos to become divisive forces.

9. Technology, Politics, and the Future of Ego

As we look to the future, emerging technologies promise to reshape the landscape of politics and power, presenting new challenges and opportunities concerning ego.

Artificial Intelligence and big data analytics are already being used to micro-target political messages, potentially worsening the echo chamber effect, and allowing for more sophisticated manipulation of voters' egos and identities.

Virtual and augmented reality technologies could revolutionise political campaigning and citizen engagement and risk creating even more immersive ego-reinforcing bubbles.

Blockchain and other decentralised technologies offer the potential for new forms of democratic participation and transparency, which could provide checks against ego-driven corruption and power concentration.

The rise of transnational digital communities and cryptocurrencies challenges traditional notions of national identity and sovereignty, potentially shifting the locus of political ego investment from the nation-state to other forms of collective identity.

As these technologies evolve, it will be crucial to guide their development and application in ways that foster healthy political engagement while mitigating the potentially harmful effects of unchecked egos.

10. Biblical Perspectives on Ego and Power

Many biblical narratives offer insights into the relationship between ego, power, and leadership that remain relevant in our current political context.

The story of King Saul in the Old Testament provides a cautionary tale about the corrupting influence of power on the ego. Saul's first humility leads to jealousy, paranoia, and a desperate clinging to power, ultimately leading to his downfall.

Conversely, despite their flaws, figures like Moses and David are often portrayed as leaders who struggle with their egos and strive to serve a higher purpose. Moses' initial reluctance to lead and his ongoing dialogue with God can be seen as a model of leadership that maintains humility in the face of great responsibility.

The teachings of Jesus in the New Testament often emphasise the importance of humility and service in leadership. For instance, washing the disciples' feet provides a powerful counter-model to ego-driven authoritarian leadership.

Proverbs and other wisdom literature in the Bible often warn against the dangers of pride and arrogance in leadership, offering timeless advice for keeping the ego in check: "Pride goes before destruction, a haughty spirit before a fall" (Proverbs 16:18).

11. Towards a Post-Ego Politics

As we conclude this chapter, we must ask: Is post-ego politics possible? If so, what might it look like?

While cutting ego from politics is unrealistic and perhaps undesirable—after all, a certain level of self-assurance and self-interest can motivate positive change—we can strive for a political culture that better balances individual ego with collective welfare.

This might involve:

1. Electoral systems that incentivise cooperation and long-term thinking over short-term ego gratification.

2. Civic education that fosters critical thinking, empathy, and understanding of diverse perspectives.

3. Media literacy programs that help citizens navigate the complex information landscape and resist ego-driven manipulation.

4. Political institutions that provide robust checks and balances against the potential excesses of individual egos.

5. Leadership development programs that cultivate humility, emotional intelligence, and a service-oriented mindset.

6. Public discourse norms that value intellectual honesty, willingness to admit mistakes and genuine engagement with opposing viewpoints.

7. Decision-making processes that incorporate diverse voices and long-term impact assessments.

Transcending ego-driven politics requires a shift in how we conceive of power—not as a tool for self-aggrandisement or domination but as a means of service and stewardship. It involves expanding our sphere of concern beyond personal or national self-interest to encompass the welfare of all humanity and the health of our shared planet.

As we navigate the complexities of 21st-century politics, the words attributed to Martin Luther King Jr. offer a powerful guidepost: "Every man must decide whether he will walk in the light of creative altruism or the darkness of destructive selfishness." In choosing the former, we open the possibility of a politics that harnesses the best human nature to address our shared challenges and create a more just, sustainable, and flourishing world for all.

CHAPTER 3: HEALTHCARE: FROM SERVICE TO INDUSTRY

1. Introduction: The Transformation of Healthcare

One of the most significant transformations in modern society is the evolution of healthcare from a primarily service-oriented profession to a massive industry. This shift has brought remarkable advancements in medical technology and treatment capabilities and troubling changes in the fundamental nature of healthcare delivery. In this chapter, we will explore how the industrialisation of healthcare has intersected with societal ego, creating a complex landscape where healing, profit, and personal ambition intertwine in often problematic ways.

We will examine this transformation through various lenses: historical developments, economic forces, technological advancements, and ethical considerations. We'll also explore how this shift has impacted patients, healthcare providers, and society. Throughout, we'll consider how the ego—both individual and collective—has shaped and been shaped by these changes.

As we navigate this complex topic, we'll also draw on biblical teachings and other ancient wisdom traditions that offer perspectives on healing, compassion, and the proper use of knowledge and power. These timeless insights may provide valuable guidance as we grapple with the challenges of modern healthcare.

2. The Historical Evolution of Healthcare

To understand the current state of healthcare, we must first look at its historical evolution. For much of human history, healthcare was primarily a community service. Healers, whether shamans, midwives, or early physicians, were integral to their societies, often combining empirical knowledge with spiritual practices.

The Hippocratic Oath, dating back to ancient Greece, established ethical standards for medical practice that emphasised the importance of patient care: "I will use treatment to help the sick according to my ability and judgment, but never with a view to injury and wrong-doing." This ethos of service remained central to healthcare for centuries.

The Scientific Revolution and Enlightenment brought significant advancements in medical knowledge and practice. The 19th century saw the rise of modern hospitals, nursing as a profession, and breakthroughs like germ theory and anaesthesia. Despite these changes, healthcare remained largely a calling rather than an industry.

The 20th century marked a turning point. Developing antibiotics, vaccines, and other medical technologies dramatically improved health outcomes. However, these advancements also came with increased costs and complexity. The rise of health insurance, first as a private industry and later with government programs like Medicare and Medicaid in the United States, began to change the economic structure of healthcare.

By the late 20th century, healthcare in many developed countries had transformed into a massive industry. In the U.S., the passage of laws allowing for-profit hospitals and the rise of pharmaceutical and medical device companies as major economic players accelerated this trend. Today, healthcare represents a significant portion of GDP in many countries, with the U.S. spending nearly 18% of its GDP on healthcare as of 2021.

This historical trajectory raises essential questions: How has the industrialisation of healthcare affected the fundamental mission of healing? Has the profit motive enhanced or detracted from the quality and accessibility of care? How has this shift impacted the ego and motivations of healthcare workers?

3. The Economics of Modern Healthcare

The transformation of healthcare into a significant industry has profound economic implications. Introducing the profit motive into healthcare delivery has created a complex system where financial incentives often compete with patient care priorities.

Healthcare has become one of the largest sectors of the economy in several countries, particularly the United States. This has created powerful vested interests—from insurance companies to hospital chains to pharmaceutical firms—significantly influencing healthcare policy and practice.

The fee-for-service model, which dominates many healthcare systems, can create perverse incentives. Providers may be motivated to perform more procedures or prescribe more medications, not necessarily because they're the best option for the patient but because they generate more revenue. This system can feed into ego-driven behaviour, where success is measured more in financial terms than in patient outcomes.

The rising healthcare costs have created a crisis of affordability in many countries. In the U.S., medical debt is a leading cause of bankruptcy, highlighting the human cost of treating healthcare primarily as a market commodity rather than a public good.

The pharmaceutical industry, in particular, has been scrutinised for pricing practices prioritising profit over accessibility. The ego-driven pursuit of blockbuster drugs and ever-increasing shareholder value has led to situations where life-saving medications are priced out of reach for many patients.

However, it's important to note that the industrialisation of healthcare has also brought benefits. The profit motive has driven innovation in medical technologies and treatments. Large-scale healthcare organisations can achieve economies of scale that smaller practices cannot, potentially reducing costs and improving efficiency.

The challenge is to balance the undeniable benefits of a dynamic, innovative healthcare sector with the ethical imperative to provide accessible, patient-centered care. This balance must also consider the role of individual and institutional ego in driving behaviour within the healthcare industry.

4. Technology and the Ego in Healthcare

Technological advancements have revolutionised healthcare, offering unprecedented disease diagnosis, treatment, and prevention capabilities. However, the relationship between technology and ego in healthcare is complex and sometimes problematic.

On the one hand, medical technology can be seen as a triumph of human ingenuity, a manifestation of our collective ego's drive to conquer disease and extend life. Cutting-edge medical devices, sophisticated imaging technologies, and breakthrough drugs represent remarkable achievements.

However, the allure of high-tech medicine can sometimes overshadow more fundamental aspects of care. The "technological imperative" in medicine—the drive to use the newest, most advanced treatments simply because they exist—can lead to overtreatment and neglect of more straightforward, often more appropriate interventions.

The ego gratification that comes from mastering complex technologies can influence medical decision-making. Surgeons might be biased towards recommending surgery over more conservative treatments, not necessarily out of financial motivation but because surgery is where their skill and ego investment lie.

While electronic health records (EHRs) offer potential benefits regarding data management and care coordination, they have also been criticised for turning doctors into data entry clerks and reducing face-to-face time with patients. This technology, intended to improve care, can paradoxically distance healthcare providers from the human aspects of their work.

Artificial Intelligence and machine learning present new frontiers in healthcare, offering the potential for more accurate diagnoses and personalised treatments. However, they also raise questions about the role of human judgment in medicine. Will the future doctor be more of a technician, interpreting AI outputs, rather than a healer relying on personal knowledge and intuition?

The rise of personal health technologies—from fitness trackers to smartphone apps that monitor various health metrics—represents a new intersection of technology, healthcare, and personal ego. While these tools can empower individuals to take charge of their health, they can also encourage obsessive self-monitoring and an overly mechanistic view of health.

As we navigate the ongoing technological revolution in healthcare, we must ask: How can we harness the power of technology while maintaining the human touch in medicine? How do we balance the ego gratification of technological mastery with the humility required for genuine patient-centred care?

5. The Pharmaceutical Industry: Innovation and Ethical Challenges

The pharmaceutical industry is at the forefront of the industrialisation of healthcare, embodying both the remarkable potential and the ethical pitfalls of profit-driven medicine. This sector has produced life-saving drugs that have transformed the treatment of many diseases, yet it has also been the subject of intense criticism for its business practices.

Drug development is lengthy, expensive, and risky. The high costs of bringing a new drug to market are often used to justify high prices. However, this model has led to a focus on "blockbuster" drugs—those that can generate billions in revenue—often at the expense of research into less profitable but potentially more needed treatments, such as new antibiotics or drugs for rare diseases.

Pharmaceutical companies' marketing practices have been particularly scrutinised. The enormous sums spent on marketing to doctors—through sales representatives, sponsored education, and direct gifts—raise questions about undue influence on prescribing practices. Direct-to-consumer advertising of prescription drugs, allowed in only a few countries, has been criticised for promoting the overuse of medications and inflating healthcare costs.

The opioid crisis in the United States provides a stark example of how the profit motive in pharmaceuticals can lead to devastating public health consequences. The aggressive marketing of opioid painkillers, downplaying their addictive potential, has been linked to hundreds of thousands of deaths.

Issues of intellectual property and drug pricing on a global scale highlight the tension between profit and public health. While patent protections incentivise innovation, they can keep drug prices high and out of reach for many patients, particularly in developing countries.

However, it is essential to recognise that the pharmaceutical industry has also been responsible for tremendous advances in human health. From vaccines that have eradicated diseases to treatments that have turned HIV from a death sentence to a manageable chronic condition, the positive impact of pharmaceutical innovation is undeniable.

The challenge lies in aligning the profit motive of the pharmaceutical industry more closely with public health needs. This might involve rethinking incentive structures, increasing public funding for essential research, and strengthening regulatory oversight to ensure that the pursuit of profit does not come at the expense of patient welfare.

6. The Changing Role of Healthcare Providers

The industrialisation of healthcare has significantly altered the role and experience of healthcare providers. Doctors, nurses, and other medical professionals have seen their work increasingly shaped by business considerations, often in ways that conflict with their training and ethical commitments.

The idea of independent physicians who run their practice and have complete autonomy in patient care decisions has given way to employed physicians working within large healthcare systems. While this shift can bring benefits in terms of resources and support, it also means that doctors must navigate corporate policies and priorities that may only sometimes align with their clinical judgment.

The pressure to see more patients in less time, driven by financial imperatives, can lead to burnout and disconnection from the core mission of healing. While intended to improve quality, focusing on metrics and performance indicators can sometimes create perverse incentives that prioritise measurable outcomes over less tangible but equally important aspects of care.

Nurses, often on the front lines of patient care, have seen their roles expand and become more technologically complex. While this can be empowering, it can also distance nurses from the bedside care that is often most meaningful to both them and their patients.

The rise of mid-level practitioners, such as nurse practitioners and physician assistants, represents a response to healthcare needs and a changing economic model. While these roles can improve access to care, they also raise questions about the nature of medical expertise and the future of the physician's role.

These changes have also impacted medical education. The prohibitive cost of medical school can saddle new doctors with substantial debt, potentially influencing their career choices towards higher-paying specialities rather than much-needed primary care roles.

The corporatisation of healthcare has introduced new power dynamics. Physicians and other providers must increasingly answer to administrators focused on the bottom line. This can create ethical dilemmas when financial considerations conflict with what providers believe is best for their patients.

However, it is essential to note that many healthcare providers have found ways to maintain their commitment to patient care within this new landscape. Movements towards patient-centred care, narrative medicine, and integrative health represent attempts to reconnect with the core values of healing within modern healthcare systems.

7. The Patient Experience in the Age of Industrialized Healthcare

The transformation of healthcare into a significant industry has profoundly affected the patient experience. While advancements in medical technology and treatments have helped patients, they have also had to navigate an increasingly complex and often impersonal healthcare system.

One of the most significant changes has been the commodification of the patient. In a system driven by financial incentives, patients sometimes feel more like customers or products than individuals seeking healing. This can manifest in rushed appointments, a focus on billable procedures, and care that feels fragmented and lacking in individualised touch.

The complexity of modern healthcare systems, particularly in countries with mixed public-private models, can be overwhelming for patients. Navigating insurance coverage, understanding treatment options, and managing multiple specialists can be a significant source of stress, often at a time when patients are already vulnerable due to illness.

The rise of patient consumerism—the idea that patients should approach healthcare as informed consumers making choices in a marketplace—has had mixed effects. While it can empower patients to be more active in their care, it can also burden individuals with making complex medical decisions without the necessary ability.

The industrialisation of healthcare has worsened health inequities in many ways. Those with financial resources and the ability to navigate complex systems often have access to better care, while vulnerable populations can be underserved or excluded.

However, there have also been positive developments for patients. The patient advocacy movement has strengthened, pushing for more patient-centred care and greater patient involvement in medical decision-making. The rise of online health information and patient communities has allowed for greater sharing of knowledge and support, although it also raises issues of misinformation.

Technological advancements have opened new possibilities for patient care, from telemedicine, which improves access to specialists, to wearable devices, which allow for continuous health monitoring. Yet, these technologies also raise questions about privacy, the medicalisation of daily life, and the potential loss of human touch in healthcare.

As we consider the future of healthcare, centring the patient experience will be crucial. How can we create systems that harness the benefits of modern medical capabilities while ensuring that care remains personal, compassionate, and accessible to all?

8. The "God Complex" and Medical Hubris

The industrialisation of healthcare, combined with remarkable advances in medical science, has sometimes led to what critics describe as a "God complex" among some medical professionals. This term refers to an inflated sense of ability, expertise, and authority that can lead to arrogance and dismissal of alternative viewpoints or approaches.

The highly specialised nature of modern medicine can contribute to this mindset. As doctors become experts in increasingly narrow fields, they tend to overestimate the scope of their knowledge and underestimate the complexity of the human body and the healing process.

The "technological imperative" in medicine - the drive to use the most advanced treatments available - can feed into this God complex. There's often an assumption that more intervention is always better, neglecting the potential for harm and overlooking the body's natural healing capacities.

This attitude can manifest in various ways:

- Dismissal of patient input: Doctors with a God complex may disregard patients' knowledge about their bodies and experiences.

- Overconfidence in diagnoses and treatments can lead to missed diagnoses or unnecessary and potentially harmful interventions.

- Resistance to admitting mistakes: A God complex can make it difficult for healthcare providers to acknowledge errors, impeding efforts to improve patient safety.

- Dismissal of alternative or complementary approaches: While healthy scepticism is essential in medicine, an inflated ego can lead to a blanket dismissal of approaches outside one's training.

The consequences of medical hubris can be severe. The history of medicine is replete with examples of harmful treatments that persisted due to professional arrogance, from bloodletting to the overuse of lobotomies.

However, it's important to note that many healthcare providers maintain a sense of humility in the face of the complexities of human health. The rise of narrative medicine, which emphasises understanding the patient's full story, and the growing recognition of the limits of the biomedical model represent pushback against the God complex in medicine.

Medical education is also evolving to address these issues, with greater emphasis on communication skills, cultural competence, and recognition of the limits of medical knowledge. The concept of "clinical humility"—maintaining an awareness of one's knowledge limitations and the potential for error—is increasingly emphasised in medical training.

As we navigate the tension between confidence and humility in medicine, we might draw wisdom from ancient teachings. The biblical proverb "Pride goes before destruction, a haughty spirit before a fall" (Proverbs 16:18) is a relevant warning against the dangers of medical hubris.

9. Alternative and Complementary Medicine: Challenge to the Status Quo

The rise of alternative and complementary medicine challenges and critiques industrialised healthcare. These approaches, which include practices like acupuncture, herbal medicine, chiropractic care, and mind-body techniques, often emphasise a more holistic view of health and healing.

The growing popularity of these modalities is a response to conventional medicine's perceived shortcomings. Patients often turn to alternative approaches when they feel that mainstream healthcare is too impersonal, too focused on symptoms rather than root causes, or too quick to prescribe drugs or invasive treatments.

The philosophy behind many alternative approaches aligns

with ancient healing traditions, which view health as a balance or harmony rather than simply the absence of disease. This perspective can offer a counterpoint to biomedicine's sometimes reductionist approach.

However, the relationship between conventional and alternative medicine is complex and often contentious. Critics of alternative medicine point to the lack of scientific evidence for many of its claims and worry that patients will forgo proven treatments in favour of unproven alternatives.

The medical establishment's response to alternative medicine has evolved. While there was initially widespread dismissal, there is growing interest in integrative medicine, which aims to combine the best of conventional and alternative approaches.

The NIH's National Center for Complementary and Integrative Health in the U.S. is an institutionalised effort to evaluate alternative therapies scientifically. This recognition that some alternative approaches may have value, even if the mechanisms aren't fully understood within the current biomedical paradigm, reflects this.

The commercialisation of alternative medicine presents its own set of challenges. As these practices have gained popularity, they've become big business, sometimes replicating the profit-driven model they initially critiqued.

From the ego perspective, the alternative medicine debate reflects a clash of paradigms and professional identities. Conventional medical professionals may feel their expertise and authority challenged, while practitioners of alternative medicine may feel dismissed and marginalised by the mainstream medical establishment.

As we move forward, the challenge is to foster a medical

landscape that integrates diverse healing approaches while maintaining scientific rigour and prioritising patient safety. This integration requires humility on all sides—a willingness to acknowledge the limitations of one's paradigm and to learn from other perspectives.

10. The Ethics of Healthcare in a Profit-Driven System

The transformation of healthcare into a significant industry has created numerous ethical dilemmas. At the heart of these issues is the fundamental question: Can the profit motive coexist with the moral imperative to provide compassionate, equitable care?

One of the most pressing ethical issues is access to care. In systems where healthcare is treated primarily as a market commodity, those without financial means may be left without essential medical services. This raises questions about healthcare as a human right versus a privilege.

The pricing of medical services and pharmaceuticals presents another ethical challenge. High prices can make treatments inaccessible to many, yet companies argue these prices are necessary to fund further research and development. How do we balance the need for innovation with the imperative to make treatments accessible?

Conflicts of interest abound in a profit-driven healthcare system. Physicians with financial stakes in medical devices or pharmaceuticals may need help balancing their economic interests with their duty to provide unbiased patient care. Similarly, hospitals may face tensions between their bottom line and providing the best care for each patient.

The issue of defensive medicine - the practice of recommending tests or treatments to avoid potential lawsuits rather than because they're medically necessary - highlights how legal and financial concerns can distort medical decision-making.

End-of-life care presents particularly complex ethical issues in a profit-driven system. There can be financial incentives to prolong life at all costs, even when this may not align with patient wishes or best practices for compassionate care.

The corporatisation of healthcare has also raised issues around patient privacy and the use of medical data. The valuable health data generated in the course of care is increasingly seen as an asset by healthcare companies, raising concerns about how this information is used and protected.

However, it's important to note that the motive for profit in healthcare isn't inherently unethical. It can drive innovation, efficiency, and improvements in care. The challenge is to create systems and incentives that align profit with ethical care and public health outcomes.

Some healthcare organisations are exploring new models that attempt to balance these concerns. For example, value-based care models aim to tie compensation to patient outcomes rather than the volume of services provided. Social impact investing in healthcare seeks to generate both financial returns and positive social outcomes.

As we grapple with these moral challenges, we might draw wisdom from various ethical frameworks. The ancient medical ethos of "First, not harm" remains a powerful guiding principle. Religious teachings on compassion and care for the vulnerable can inform approaches to healthcare equity. Philosophical frameworks like utilitarianism or Kantian ethics can provide tools for navigating complex ethical trade-offs.

Addressing the ethical challenges of profit-driven healthcare will require ongoing dialogue, strong regulatory frameworks, and a commitment to placing patient welfare at the centre of all healthcare decisions.

11. The Global Perspective: Healthcare Disparities and the Role of Ego

While much of our discussion has focused on healthcare in developed countries, it's crucial to consider the global perspective on healthcare industrialisation. The stark disparities in healthcare access and outcomes between wealthy and less wealthy nations highlight the ethical challenges of a worldwide healthcare system heavily influenced by market forces.

In many developing countries, essential healthcare services still need to be within reach of sizeable portions of the population. The profit-driven healthcare and pharmaceutical development model often neglects to pay more attention to these populations' needs, as they are not seen as lucrative.

The "issue brain drain" in healthcare, where medical professionals from developing countries are recruited to work in wealthier nations, worsens these disparities. This trend, driven in part by the allure of higher salaries and better working conditions, can leave poorer countries with critical shortages of healthcare providers.

While often well-intentioned, global health initiatives can sometimes reflect an institutional ego. Imposing Western medical models without adequately considering local cultural contexts and healthcare practices can be seen as medical imperialism.

The COVID-19 pandemic has starkly illustrated these global disparities, particularly in the development and distribution of vaccines. The phenomenon of "vaccine nationalism," where wealthy countries prioritise their populations over global needs, reflects how national ego can override considerations of international public health.

However, there are also positive trends in global health. Organisations like Doctors Without Borders show a healthcare delivery model that transcends national boundaries and profit motives. The success of global health initiatives in areas like HIV treatment and vaccine distribution for childhood diseases shows the potential for coordinated international action.

The "reverse innovation" concept in healthcare, where low-cost solutions developed for resource-poor settings are adapted for use in wealthy countries, offers a model for more equitable global health innovation. This approach challenges the assumption that medical advancement must flow from rich to poor countries.

As we consider the future of global healthcare, key questions emerge: How can we create systems that provide quality healthcare for all, regardless of ability to pay or accident of birth? How can we harness the healthcare industry's innovative potential to address global health challenges while ensuring equitable access to benefits?

12. The Future of Healthcare: Balancing Innovation, Ethics, and Equity

As we look to the future of healthcare, we face the challenge of harnessing the benefits of industrialisation and technological advancement while mitigating its negative impacts. Several trends and possibilities appear:

Personalised Medicine: Advances in genetics and significant data analytics promise to enable more tailored, effective treatments. However, this also raises concerns about genetic privacy and the potential for new forms of discrimination.

Artificial Intelligence in Healthcare: AI can improve the efficiency of diagnostics, treatment planning, and health systems. Yet, it also raises questions about the role of human judgment in medicine and the potential for algorithmic bias.

Telemedicine and Digital Health: The COVID-19 pandemic accelerated the adoption of telemedicine, which can improve access to care, particularly in underserved areas. However, it also risks exacerbating the digital divide in healthcare.

Value-Based Care: Models that tie provider compensation to patient outcomes rather than the volume of services could help align financial incentives with quality care.

Patient Empowerment: Continued growth in patient advocacy and shared decision-making models could help balance the power dynamics in healthcare.

Global Health Equity: Increased recognition of health as a global public good could drive more coordinated international efforts to address health disparities.

Integrative Health: Greater integration of alternative and complementary approaches with conventional medicine could lead to more holistic, patient-centred care models.

<u>As we navigate these changes, several key principles may guide us:</u>

1. Prioritizing Patient Welfare: Regardless of the business model or technology used, the fundamental purpose of healthcare - to heal and alleviate suffering - must remain paramount.

2. Equity and Access: Efforts must be made to ensure that advancements in healthcare benefit all segments of society, not just those who can afford to pay.

3. Ethical Innovation: New technologies and treatments should be developed and implemented with careful consideration of their ethical implications.

4. Balancing Specialization and Holistic Care: While specialised expertise is crucial, it must be balanced with a holistic understanding of patient health.

5. Sustainable Healthcare: The environmental impact of healthcare systems must be considered, and models that are sustainable for human and planetary health must be promoted.

6. Global Cooperation: Addressing global health challenges will require unprecedented international cooperation and resource sharing.

7. Humanizing Healthcare: Despite technological advancements, the human elements of care—compassion, communication, and personal touch—must be preserved and emphasised.

13. Conclusion: Rediscovering the Heart of Healing

As we conclude our exploration of the industrialisation of healthcare, we return to the fundamental question: How can we harness the undeniable benefits of modern medical advances and efficient healthcare systems while staying true to the core mission of healing?

The transformation of healthcare into a significant industry has brought remarkable advancements in our ability to diagnose and treat disease. It has also driven innovation, expanded our understanding of human health, and, in many ways, improved healthcare outcomes. Yet, it has also created a system often characterised by impersonal care, inequitable access, and ethical dilemmas.

The challenge is not to dismantle the healthcare industry but to reorient it more firmly around the values that have always been at the heart of the healing professions. This reorientation requires grappling with the role of individual and institutional ego in healthcare.

For individual healthcare providers, this means cultivating a balance between the confidence necessary to make complex decisions and the humility to recognise the limits of one's knowledge and the importance of patient welfare. It means resisting the allure of the "God complex" and embracing the partnership model with patients.

For healthcare institutions, it means finding ways to align financial sustainability with ethical, patient-centred care. It means creating cultures that value compassion and holistic care as much as technological advancement and efficiency.

For society, it means engaging in ongoing dialogue about our healthcare priorities. It means grappling with tough questions about resource allocation, the limits of medical intervention, and the balance between individual and public health needs.

Ancient wisdom traditions might inspire us as we navigate these challenges. The biblical injunction to "Love your neighbour as yourself" (Leviticus 19:18) provides an ethical foundation that transcends any healthcare system or technology. The Hippocratic tradition's emphasis on the patient's welfare offers a constant touchstone for medical decision-making.

We might also look to modern pioneers who have found ways to provide compassionate, effective care within (and sometimes despite) industrialised healthcare systems. From physicians pioneering new primary care models to nurses leading initiatives in patient-centred care to community health workers bridging gaps in underserved areas, there are numerous examples of individuals and organisations rediscovering the heart of healing.

Ultimately, the future of healthcare lies not just in scientific breakthroughs or system redesigns but in a renewed commitment to medicine's fundamental purpose: to heal, comfort, and care. By keeping this purpose at the centre of all our efforts—whether we are developing new drugs, implementing health policies, or providing direct patient care—we can work towards a future where the industrialisation of healthcare serves, rather than subverts, the timeless mission of healing.

In this endeavour, we must remain vigilant against the excesses of ego - the temptation to prioritise profit over people, technology over touch, or professional status over patient needs. Instead, we must cultivate a collective ego that takes pride not in power or profit but in our capacity to alleviate suffering and promote health for all.

The industrialisation of healthcare has brought us to a crossroads. The path we choose will decide not just the future of medicine but, in many ways, the future of our society. By recommitting to the core values of healing, fostering systems that balance innovation with compassion, and ensuring that the benefits of medical progress are equitably shared, we can create a healthcare system that truly serves humanity in all its diversity and complexity.

As we move forward, let us carry with us the wisdom of the past, the knowledge of the present, and a vision of a future where healthcare is not just an industry but a manifestation of our highest aspirations as a society. In this future, every individual can access the care they need to live healthy, dignified lives regardless of their circumstances. In this way, we can transform the industrialisation of healthcare from a challenge to be managed into an opportunity to elevate the practice of medicine and the health of our global community.

CHAPTER 4: CONSUMERISM AND THE CULT OF SELF

1. Introduction: The Rise of Consumer Culture

Few threads are as pervasive and influential as consumerism in the tapestry of modern society. What began as a simple economic model of goods and services exchange has evolved into a powerful force shaping our identities, values, and social interactions. This chapter explores the intricate relationship between consumerism and the cult of self, examining how the relentless pursuit of material goods and experiences has become intertwined with our sense of identity and self-worth.

As we delve into this topic, we will trace the historical development of consumer culture, analyse its psychological underpinnings, and examine its far-reaching impacts on individuals, communities, and the environment. We will also explore how consumerism intersects with technology, media, and globalisation, creating a complex web of influences that shape our desires and behaviours.

Throughout this exploration, we will consider how consumerism's ethos often starkly contrasts traditional wisdom and spiritual teachings, including those found in the Bible and other ancient texts. These timeless perspectives offer valuable counterpoints to consumer culture's often short-sighted and ego-driven nature.

Our journey through this topic will be critical and nuanced, recognising that while consumerism has brought certain benefits and comforts, it has also contributed to significant social and environmental challenges. By understanding consumerism's mechanisms and consequences, we can envision alternatives that lead to more fulfilling, sustainable, and equitable ways of living.

2. Historical Context: From Necessity to Excess

To understand consumerism's current state, we must first examine its historical roots. The concept of consuming goods and services is as old as human civilisation, but the form of consumerism that dominates modern society is a recent phenomenon.

Pre-industrial societies focused on subsistence, with most people producing what they needed for survival. Trade existed but was limited and often based on necessity rather than desire. The Industrial Revolution of the 18th and 19th centuries marked a significant shift, as mass production techniques made goods more widely available and affordable.

The 20th century saw the birth of modern consumer culture, particularly in the United States. The 1920s, often called the "Roaring Twenties," saw a boom in consumer goods and the rise of advertising as a significant industry. This period also marked the beginning of consumer credit, which allowed people to purchase goods beyond their immediate means.

The post-World War II era was pivotal in developing consumer culture. In the United States and much of the Western world, economic prosperity, suburban expansion, and the rise of mass media created the perfect conditions for consumerism to flourish. The American Dream became increasingly defined by material possessions—a car in every driveway and a television in every living room.

The 1950s and 1960s saw the rise of youth culture as a significant market force, with teenagers and young adults becoming essential consumers. This period also saw critiques of consumer culture appear, with books like Vance Packard's The Hidden Persuaders (1957) exposing the advertising industry's manipulative techniques.

The late 20th century brought globalisation and the digital revolution, further transforming consumer culture. The rise of multinational corporations, global brands, and e-commerce created a truly global marketplace. At the same time, the environmental and social costs of unchecked consumerism became increasingly evident, leading to the growth of movements advocating for ethical and sustainable consumption.

Today, we find ourselves in what some scholars call "hyperconsumerism," where consumption goes far beyond meeting basic needs and becomes a central aspect of identity formation and social interaction. This historical trajectory raises essential questions: How did we move from a culture of necessity to one of excess? What societal and psychological shifts enabled this transformation? And what are the consequences of this shift for individuals, society, and the planet?

3. The Psychology of Consumerism: Desire, Identity, and the Self

At the heart of modern consumerism lies a complex web of psychological factors that drive our purchasing behaviours and connect our consumption habits to our sense of self. Understanding these psychological mechanisms is crucial to grasping the power and persistence of consumer culture.

One key concept is symbolic consumption. In consumer societies, goods and services are not merely functional items but carriers of meaning. We consume products and their associated ideas, values, and identities. A luxury car isn't just a mode of transportation; it's a symbol of success and status. A particular clothing brand isn't just about covering our bodies; it's a statement about who we are or aspire to be.

This symbolic aspect of consumption ties closely to the concept of the "extended self," developed by consumer behaviour researcher Russell Belk. This theory suggests that we view our possessions as part of our identity, extensions of our self. In this way, consumption becomes a means of self-expression and self-creation.

The role of advertising and marketing in shaping consumer psychology cannot be overstated. These industries have become incredibly sophisticated in creating and manipulating desire. By tapping into our deepest fears, aspirations, and insecurities, advertisers create a perpetual sense of lack that consumption can only fill (temporarily).

The concept of "retail therapy"—the idea that shopping can improve one's mood—points to the emotional aspect of consumption. Many people turn to shopping to cope with stress, sadness, or other negative emotions. While this can provide a short-term boost, it often leads to a cycle of temporary highs followed by guilt or emptiness, driving further consumption.

The social comparison theory, developed by psychologist Leon Festinger, helps explain the competitive aspect of consumerism. We often judge our success and worth by comparing ourselves to others, and in a consumer society, this comparison frequently occurs through the lens of material possessions and lifestyle.

The psychology of scarcity and abundance also plays a role in consumer behaviour. Marketers often create a sense of scarcity (limited-time offers, exclusive products) to drive desire and purchasing behaviour. Paradoxically, the abundance of choices in modern consumer societies can lead to decision fatigue and dissatisfaction, as outlined in Barry Schwartz's concept of the "paradox of choice."

The rise of social media has added new dimensions to the psychology of consumerism. Platforms like Instagram and Pinterest create endless opportunities for social comparison and lifestyle aspiration while turning users into brands that others consume.

Understanding these psychological mechanisms can help us see how deeply consumerism is embedded in our sense of self and social interactions. It raises crucial questions: How can we find authentic sources of identity and self-worth beyond consumption? How can we foster psychological well-being in a culture that constantly tells us we are insufficient?

4. Advertising: The Engine of Desire

Advertising is the primary engine driving consumer culture. It plays a crucial role in shaping our desires, influencing our self-perception, and ultimately guiding our purchasing decisions. The evolution of advertising from simple product announcements to sophisticated, multi-platform campaigns reflects the growing complexity of consumer culture itself.

The early days of modern advertising in the late 19th and early 20th centuries focused primarily on informing consumers about product features and benefits. However, by the mid-20th century, advertisers shifted towards more emotional and psychological appeals. The work of psychologists like Ernest

Dichter, who applied Freudian psychoanalysis to consumer behaviour, marked a turning point in advertising strategy.

Today's advertising industry employs a wide array of psychological techniques to create and manipulate desire:

1. Emotional Appeals: Advertisements often associate products with positive emotions or desirable states of being, such as happiness, success, belonging, or excitement.

2. Fear and Insecurity: Many ads play on our fears and insecurities, positioning products as solutions to perceived personal or social inadequacies.

3. Lifestyle Association: Products are often presented not in terms of their functional benefits but as gateways to desirable lifestyles or social groups.

4. Celebrity Endorsement: By associating products with admired public figures, advertisers tap into our desire for status and our tendency to emulate those we admire.

5. Scarcity and Exclusivity: Creating a sense that a rare or exclusive product can drive desire and purchasing behaviour.

6. Social Proof: Showing that "everyone" is using a product taps into our social instincts and fear of missing out.

7. Personalization: Advanced data analytics allow for highly targeted advertising, creating the illusion of personal relevance.

The rise of digital and social media advertising has dramatically changed the landscape. Advertisers now have unprecedented access to personal data, allowing for micro-targeted campaigns. Native advertising and influencer marketing blur the lines between content and advertising, making it increasingly difficult for consumers to distinguish between genuine recommendations and paid promotions.

The pervasiveness of advertising in modern life raises significant ethical questions. Critics argue that the constant barrage of advertising creates artificial needs, promotes materialism, and contributes to psychological distress. Advertisers' targeting of children is particularly controversial, with concerns about exploiting young minds not yet capable of critical evaluation.

Moreover, the environmental impact of advertising-driven consumerism is increasingly recognised as unsustainable. By constantly promoting the acquisition of new products, advertising contributes to a culture of disposability and waste.

However, defenders of advertising argue that it plays a crucial role in a market economy by informing consumers about products and driving economic growth. They also point to advertising's role in funding media and cultural products.

As we navigate this complex landscape, several questions emerge: How can we develop greater critical awareness of advertising's influence on our desires and self-perception? What ethical guidelines should govern advertising practices? And how might we reimagine advertising's role in a more sustainable and equitable economy?

5. The Environmental Cost of Consumerism

The relentless pursuit of ever-increasing consumption has come at a staggering environmental cost. By transforming the natural world into products to be consumed, we've created ecological crises on multiple fronts.

Climate Change: Consumer goods' production, transportation, and disposal are major contributors to greenhouse gas emissions. Fast fashion, electronics, and the auto industry are particularly significant sources of carbon emissions.

Resource Depletion: Our current consumption rates are depleting natural resources at an unsustainable pace. From minerals used in electronics to water used in manufacturing, we're using Earth's finite resources faster than they can be replenished.

Waste and Pollution: The culture of disposability inherent in modern consumerism has led to massive waste problems. Landfills overflow, oceans fill with plastic, and toxic waste from manufacturing processes pollutes air, water, and soil.

Biodiversity Loss: The expansion of agriculture, mining, and urban development to meet consumer demands is destroying natural habitats and contributing to what scientists call the "sixth mass extinction."

Planned Obsolescence: Many products are designed to have artificially short lifespans, which encourages frequent replacement and contributes to waste.

The globalisation of consumer culture has exported these environmental problems worldwide. As developing countries aspire to Western consumption patterns, the ecological strain on the planet intensifies.

However, awareness of these issues is growing, leading to various responses:

1. Sustainable Consumption: A movement towards buying less but buying better - choosing products that are durable, repairable, and produced in environmentally responsible ways.

2. Circular Economy: This model eliminates waste and maximises resource use through recycling, reusing, and repurposing.

3. Minimalism: A lifestyle and design movement that emphasises living with less, countering the excesses of consumer culture.

4. Eco-Innovation: Developments in technology and design that aim to create more sustainable products and production processes.

5. Environmental Regulations: Governments are increasingly implementing policies to mitigate the environmental impacts of consumption, such as carbon pricing and bans on single-use plastics.

The environmental costs of consumerism force us to confront tough questions: How can we balance material comfort with ecological responsibility? Can we create economic systems that don't rely on ever-increasing consumption? How do we shift cultural values away from materialism towards sustainability?

6. Social and Psychological Impacts of Consumer Culture

While consumerism has brought certain comforts and conveniences, it has also had profound, often negative, impacts on social structures and individual psychological well-being.

Social Atomization: The emphasis on individual consumption can erode community ties. When identity and status are primarily expressed through purchases rather than social roles or community involvement, this can lead to increased isolation and weakening of the social fabric.

Inequality and Social Division: Consumerism often worsens social inequalities. The pressure to consume at certain levels to support social status can lead to financial stress for many. In contrast, the visible disparities in consumption between different social groups can heighten social tensions.

Work-Life Imbalance: The desire to maintain certain consumption levels often drives people to work longer hours, leading to stress, burnout, and neglect of personal relationships and non-material aspects of life.

Materialism and Well-being: Numerous psychological studies have found correlations between highly materialistic values and decreased life satisfaction, increased rates of anxiety and depression, and lower-quality relationships.

Identity Crisis: When self-worth becomes too closely tied to consumption and material possessions, it can lead to a fragile sense of identity. This can result in constant anxiety about status and a never-ending quest for validation through purchases.

The commodification of Experience: In advanced consumer societies, even experiences (travel, education, relationships) can become commodified, potentially stripping them of more profound meaning and turning them into items to be consumed and displayed.

Cultural Homogenization: Global consumer culture can flatten cultural differences as global brands and products replace local traditions and practices.

Debt and Financial Stress: Easy credit and the pressure to consume often lead to high levels of personal debt, which causes significant stress and limits future opportunities.

<u>However, it's important to note that consumer culture has also had some positive social impacts:</u>

1. Improved Standards of Living: Access to a wide range of goods has improved the quality of life for many people.

2. Cultural Exchange: Global trade has facilitated cultural exchange and increased exposure to diverse ideas and practices.

3. Consumer Activism: Ethical consumption movements have raised awareness about social and environmental issues and pressured companies to improve their practices.

4. Innovation: Consumer demand drives innovation in products and services, sometimes leading to genuine improvements in quality of life.

As we consider these impacts, key questions emerge: How can we retain the benefits of consumer society while mitigating its adverse effects? Can we create cultural narratives and social structures that emphasise less consumption and more community, creativity, and personal growth?

7. Digital Consumerism: The New Frontier

The digital revolution has dramatically reshaped the landscape of consumerism, creating new products, new ways of consuming, and new challenges for individuals and society.

E-commerce has transformed the retail experience, offering unprecedented convenience and choice. Online marketplaces like Amazon have become dominant forces, changing how we shop and our expectations about availability and delivery speed.

Digital goods and services have created new consumption categories, from streaming media to cloud storage. These intangible products challenge traditional notions of ownership and value.

Social media platforms have become powerful drivers of consumer behaviour. "Influencer" marketing turns individual users into brand ambassadors, while features like Instagram's shopping tags blur the lines between social interaction and commercial activity.

The attention economy treats user engagement as a commodity, with tech companies competing fiercely for our time and attention. This has led to concerns about addictive design in digital products and the commodification of human attention.

Big data and AI have enabled hyper-personalized marketing, with companies able to tailor their offerings based on incredibly detailed consumer profiles. While this can lead to more relevant products and services, it also raises significant privacy concerns.

The sharing economy, epitomised by companies like Uber and Airbnb, has created new consumption models based on access rather than ownership. While this can lead to more efficient resource use, it also raises questions about labour rights and the nature of ownership in the digital age.

Digital consumerism has also created new forms of conspicuous consumption. Social media platforms provide unprecedented opportunities to display purchases and experiences, intensifying social comparison and status anxiety.

However, digital technologies also offer potential solutions to some of the excesses of consumer culture:

1. Collaborative Consumption: Digital platforms enable sharing and bartering, potentially reducing overall consumption.

2. Information Transparency: Consumers can easily access information about product sourcing, manufacturing conditions, and environmental impact, enabling more ethical

consumption choices.

3. Digital Minimalism: A movement advocating for more intentional use of digital technologies, pushing back against the excesses of digital consumption.

4. Virtual and Augmented Reality: These technologies could satisfy some consumer desires (like the desire for novel experiences) with less material consumption.

As we navigate this new frontier of consumerism, important questions arise: How do we balance the conveniences of digital consumption with concerns about privacy, addiction, and the commodification of attention? How can we harness digital technologies to promote more sustainable and fulfilling forms of consumption?

8. Globalization and the Spread of Consumer Culture

The phenomenon of "glocalisation" - where global products are adapted to local tastes and cultures - demonstrates the complex interplay between international and regional forces in consumer culture. For example, McDonald's offers different menu items in various countries to cater to local preferences.

The global spread of consumer culture has had significant environmental implications. As more of the world's population adopts high-consumption lifestyles, the strain on the planet's resources intensifies. This raises difficult questions about global equity and sustainability - can the Earth support a global population consuming at the levels seen in the most affluent countries?

Critics argue that the globalisation of consumer culture leads to cultural homogenisation, eroding local traditions and diversity. However, others point out that globalisation can also lead to cultural hybridisation and new forms of creativity.

Expanding global supply chains to meet consumer demands has raised labour rights issues and working conditions in developing countries. Campaigns against "sweatshop" labour have heightened awareness of the human costs behind many consumer goods.

At the same time, globalisation has facilitated the spread of alternative consumer movements. Fairtrade, ethical consumption and sustainability initiatives now operate globally.

Digital platforms have accelerated the globalisation of consumer culture, allowing instant global communication and e-commerce that transcends national boundaries. This has created new opportunities for small producers to reach international markets and intensified competition.

As we consider the global dimensions of consumer culture, key questions emerge: How can we create a more equitable and sustainable global economy? How do we balance cultural exchange with the preservation of local traditions? And how might we envision forms of globalisation that aren't primarily driven by consumerism?

9. Consumerism and Spirituality: A Complex Relationship

The relationship between consumerism and spirituality is complex and often contradictory. Many spiritual and religious traditions emphasise values that seem at odds with consumer culture: simplicity, non-attachment to material possessions and focus on inner rather than outer wealth. Yet, consumerism has found ways to commodify spirituality, while some religious movements have embraced consumerist values.

Many religious texts warn against the dangers of materialism. The Bible, for instance, cautions that "the love of money is a root of all kinds of evil" (1 Timothy 6:10). Jesus teaches that "life does not consist in an abundance of possessions" (Luke 12:15). Similar sentiments can be found in Buddhist teachings on non-attachment, Islamic prohibitions on excess, and Hindu concepts of renunciation.

However, the "prosperity gospel" movement in Christianity starkly contrasts these traditional teachings. This theology, which suggests that financial blessing is God's will for believers, has been criticised for aligning too closely with consumerist values.

The commodification of spirituality is evident in the booming market for self-help books, meditation apps, yoga accessories, and other spiritual paraphernalia. While these products can serve as helpful tools for spiritual practice, critics argue that they often reduce complex spiritual traditions to consumable lifestyle accessories.

The concept of "spiritual materialism," introduced by Tibetan Buddhist teacher Chögyam Trungpa, describes the tendency to turn spiritual practice into a project of ego enhancement. This can manifest in the accumulation of spiritual experiences or credentials as a form of status symbol.

However, some argue that there needn't be an inherent conflict between spirituality and certain forms of consumption. Conscious consumption - making mindful choices about what we buy and why - can be seen as a spiritual practice.

Moreover, some spiritual communities are at the forefront of sustainable and ethical consumption movements, seeing environmental and social responsibility as extensions of their spiritual values.

The minimalist movement, which advocates for reducing material possessions to focus on what's truly important, can be seen as a secular approach to traditional spiritual teachings on simplicity and non-attachment.

As we navigate the intersection of consumerism and spirituality, important questions arise: How can spiritual practices help us develop healthier relationships with material possessions? Can consumption itself be approached in a more mindful, spiritual way? And how do we balance material comfort with spiritual growth?

10. The Role of Education in Consumer Society

Education plays a crucial role in shaping how individuals interact with consumer culture. From early childhood through higher education, the messages we receive about consumption, success, and the role of material goods in our lives can have lasting impacts.

In many education systems, there's an implicit (and sometimes explicit) link between education and future earning potential. This can reinforce the idea that the primary purpose of learning is to become a more effective consumer.

Marketing to children and teenagers in educational settings - through sponsored materials, vending machines, or branded events - has been a contentious issue. Critics argue that schools should be commercial-free zones, while others contend that such marketing provides needed funds for cash-strapped schools.

Financial literacy education is increasingly recognised as necessary, but there are debates about what this should entail. Should it focus narrowly on personal finance management or include broader critiques of consumer culture and the current economic system?

Media literacy education can be crucial in helping

students critically analyse advertising and resist manipulative marketing techniques. However, the rapid evolution of digital marketing presents ongoing challenges for educators who must keep pace.

Some schools have implemented programs focused on sustainability and ethical consumption to cultivate more conscious consumers. These might include lessons on the environmental impacts of consumption, Fair Trade, or the social implications of supply chains.

Higher education has increasingly been treated as a consumer good, with students often viewed as customers and education as a product. This shift has significant implications for the nature of learning and the mission of educational institutions.

Alternative educational models, such as Waldorf or Montessori schools, often place less emphasis on material rewards and more on intrinsic motivation and holistic development. These approaches might offer insights for developing educational practices that are less aligned with consumerist values.

As we consider the role of education in consumer society, key questions emerge: How can we educate young people to be informed, critical consumers without reinforcing materialistic values? What role should schools play in shaping students' relationships with consumer culture? And how might we reimagine education to prioritise human flourishing over consumer competence?

11. Consumerism and Gender: Shaping Identities and Expectations

Consumer culture intersects with gender in complex and often problematic ways, shaping expectations, identities, and behaviours along gendered lines.

Historically, women have been the primary targets of consumer advertising, reflecting and reinforcing traditional gender roles that positioned women as homemakers and primary shoppers for the family. While this has evolved, gendered marketing is still pervasive.

The beauty and fashion industries are particularly notable for their gendered marketing and its impacts on body image and self-esteem. Women, in particular, are often sold products based on created insecurities about their appearance.

Concepts of masculinity have also been shaped by consumer culture, with certain products (like cars, alcohol, or sports gear) marketed as symbols of manhood. This can reinforce narrow, potentially harmful notions of what it means to be a man.

The "pink tax" - the phenomenon where products marketed to women often cost more than comparable products for men - highlights how gender disparities are built into consumer markets.

Consumer culture often reinforces gender binaries, with products coded as "for men" or "for women." This can be particularly challenging for individuals who do not conform to traditional gender categories.

<u>However, there are also trends pushing against these gendered patterns of consumption:</u>

1. Gender-neutral marketing and product design is becoming more common, particularly in children's products.

2. Some brands are challenging traditional gender roles in their advertising, showing men in caregiving roles or women in traditionally male-dominated fields.

3. The body positivity movement pushes back against narrow

beauty standards promoted by many consumer industries.

As we examine the relationship between consumerism and gender, important questions arise: How can we promote more inclusive, less stereotypical marketing and product design forms? How do we balance the positive aspects of gendered products (which can affirm gender identity for some) with the need to avoid reinforcing limiting stereotypes? And how might we envision a consumer culture that allows for more fluid, diverse gender expressions?

12. The Future of Consumerism: Challenges and Possibilities

Looking to the future, current consumption patterns are environmentally and socially unsustainable. Yet consumerism is deeply embedded in our economic systems and cultural values. What might the future of consumption look like, and how might we transition to more sustainable and fulfilling ways of living?

<u>Several trends and possibilities appear:</u>

Sustainable Consumption: There is growing interest in environmentally sustainable and socially responsible products and services. This could lead to a shift in consumption patterns from quantity to quality.

Circular Economy: Models emphasising reusing, repairing, and recycling products could reduce waste and resource use while meeting consumer needs.

Sharing Economy: Platforms that enable the sharing of goods and services could reduce individual consumption while supporting access to needed resources.

Degrowth Movement: This economic and social philosophy advocates reducing production and consumption for ecological sustainability and social justice.

Experiential Consumption: A shift towards valuing experiences over material goods could reduce environmental impact while offering more fulfilling consumption forms.

Digital and Virtual Consumption: As more aspects of life move online, we might shift towards consuming digital goods and services, which could have a lower environmental impact.

Conscious Consumption: Increased awareness of the impacts of consumption could lead to more mindful, intentional purchasing decisions.

Localism: A move towards local production and consumption could reduce transportation costs and strengthen community ties.

Post-Scarcity Technologies: Advances in renewable energy, 3D printing, and synthetic biology could fundamentally change the nature of scarcity and abundance.

However, significant challenges remain:

1. Overcoming the growth imperative in our current economic system.

2. Addressing global inequalities in consumption levels.

3. Shifting cultural values away from materialism.

4. Balancing consumer choice with sustainability imperatives.

5. Navigating the political challenges of regulating consumption.

As we contemplate the future of consumerism, key questions emerge: How can we create economic systems that provide for human needs without relying on ever-increasing consumption? How do we balance individual freedom with collective responsibility in our consumption choices? And how might we cultivate forms of identity and meaning that aren't primarily based on what we consume?

13. Conclusion: Transcending the Consumer Self

As we conclude our exploration of consumerism and the cult of self, we're left with a complex picture. Consumer culture has brought undeniable comforts and conveniences, expanded our horizons, and improved the material quality of life for millions in many ways. Yet it has also contributed to environmental degradation, social atomisation, and a sense of perpetual dissatisfaction that seems built into its very structure.

The challenge is not to eliminate consumption—a necessary part of human existence—but to transform our relationship with it. This transformation requires us to grapple with fundamental questions about the nature of self, the sources of meaning and fulfilment in life, and our responsibilities to each other and the planet.

Moving beyond the consumer self doesn't mean rejecting material comfort or the innovations that have improved our lives. Instead, it involves developing a more balanced, conscious, and sustainable approach to consumption. It means recognising that while material goods have their place, they are not the primary source of identity, status, or happiness.

This shift requires action on multiple levels:

Individual: Cultivating mindfulness about our consumption habits, exploring sources of fulfilment beyond material acquisition, and making conscious choices about what and how we consume.

Cultural: Challenging narratives equating success and

worth with material possessions and creating new stories emphasising community, creativity, and connection to nature.

Economic: Developing new financial models prioritising well-being and sustainability over growth and profit.

Political: Implementing policies that incentivise sustainable consumption and hold producers responsible for the entire lifecycle of their products.

Educational: Teaching critical thinking skills to navigate consumer culture and fostering values beyond materialism.

Technological: Harnessing innovations to create more sustainable and fulfilling ways of meeting human needs and desires.

As we undertake this transformation, we might draw wisdom from various sources. Ancient spiritual traditions remind us of the transient nature of material possessions and the importance of inner wealth. Indigenous cultures offer models of more harmonious relationships with the natural world. Modern psychology provides insights into the roots of happiness and well-being that often have little to do with consumption.

Ultimately, transcending the consumer self involves reconnecting with aspects of our humanity that consumer culture often neglects or commodifies—our capacity for creativity, our need for genuine human connection, our sense of wonder at the natural world, and our desire to contribute to something larger than ourselves.

In doing so, we open the possibility of a future where consumption serves human flourishing rather than driving it, where our identities are built on our characters and contributions rather than our possessions, and where we measure progress not by what we have but by who we are and how we relate to each other and the world around us.

This journey beyond the consumer self is challenging. It requires us to question deeply ingrained habits, resist powerful cultural messages, and imagine new ways of living and organising our societies. But by embarking on this journey, we create the potential for more authentic, fulfilling, and sustainable ways of being—both for ourselves and the generations to come.

As we move forward, let us remember the words often attributed to Mahatma Gandhi: "There is enough in the world for everyone's need, but not for everyone's greed." In this spirit, we can work towards a future where consumption is guided by wisdom, moderation, and a deep sense of our interconnectedness with all life.

CHAPTER 5: THE PROMISE AND PERIL OF AI

1. Introduction: The AI Revolution

Artificial Intelligence (AI) is one of the most transformative technologies of our time. It promises to reshape every aspect of human society, from healthcare and education to transportation and entertainment. AI's potential applications seem boundless. Yet, as with any powerful technology, AI brings with it great promise and significant perils.

In this chapter, we will explore the multifaceted nature of AI, examining its current state, potential future developments, and the profound ethical and societal implications it raises. We will delve into how AI represents both an extension of human capabilities and a possible amplification of the human ego. We will consider how this technology might shape our understanding of intelligence, consciousness, and what it means to be human.

As we navigate this complex landscape, we will draw upon insights from computer science, philosophy, ethics, and ancient wisdom traditions, including biblical perspectives. These diverse viewpoints can offer valuable guidance as we grapple with AI's unprecedented challenges and opportunities.

Our exploration will be critical and nuanced. We recognise that AI is neither a panacea for all human problems nor an inevitable harbinger of doom. Instead, it is a powerful tool whose ultimate impact will be decided by how we develop and deploy it.

Understanding AI's mechanisms, potential, and risks can help us harness its capabilities to augment human flourishing while mitigating its potential negative consequences. This chapter aims to provide a comprehensive overview of AI, equipping readers with the knowledge and perspectives needed to engage thoughtfully with one of our era's most important technological developments.

2. Understanding AI: From Narrow to General Intelligence

Understanding AI and how it works is crucial for grasping its implications. At its core, AI refers to computer systems capable of performing tasks that typically require human intelligence. However, the field encompasses a wide range of approaches and capabilities.

Narrow or Weak AI is the type of AI currently available. It's designed to perform specific tasks within a limited domain. Examples include voice assistants like Siri or Alexa, image recognition software, and game-playing AI like AlphaGo. While these systems can outperform humans in their specific domains, they need more general intelligence and can transfer their skills to other tasks.

Machine Learning is a subset of AI that involves algorithms that can learn from and make predictions or decisions based on data. Deep learning, a type of machine learning inspired by the structure of the human brain, has driven many recent AI breakthroughs, particularly in areas like natural language processing and computer vision.

General AI (AGI) refers to AI systems that possess human-like general intelligence and are capable of understanding, learning, and applying knowledge across a wide range of tasks. AGI remains a theoretical concept, and there is significant debate about when or if it might be achieved.

<u>Superintelligent AI:</u> This hypothetical form of AI would surpass human intelligence across all domains. While purely speculative at this point, the possibility of superintelligent AI raises profound questions about the future of humanity.

Several key factors have driven the development of AI:

1. **Increased computing power**: Modern hardware, particularly GPUs (Graphics Processing Units), has enabled the processing vast amounts of data necessary for complex AI algorithms.

2. **Big Data:** The explosion of digital data has provided the raw material for training sophisticated AI models.

3. **Algorithmic advances:** Breakthroughs in areas like deep learning have dramatically improved AI capabilities.

4. **Cloud computing:** The ability to distribute AI processing across networks of computers has accelerated development and deployment.

As we consider the future of AI, key questions emerge: How close are we to achieving AGI, and what would be the implications? How can we ensure that AI development aligns with human values and ethics? And how might the evolution of AI change our understanding of intelligence itself?

3. AI in Daily Life: Current Applications and Future Possibilities

AI has already become integral to many people's daily

lives, often in ways that are not immediately apparent. Understanding these current applications provides a foundation for considering future possibilities.

Current Applications:

1. **Virtual Assistants:** AI-powered assistants like Siri, Alexa, and Google Assistant have become commonplace, helping with tasks from setting reminders to controlling smart home devices.

2. **Recommendation Systems:** Services like Netflix, Spotify, and Amazon use AI to personalise recommendations based on user behaviour.

3. **Social Media:** AI algorithms curate content feeds, detect inappropriate content, and target advertisements.

4. **Transportation:** AI is crucial in navigation apps, ride-sharing services, and the development of autonomous vehicles.

5. **Healthcare:** AI assists in diagnosing diseases, analysing medical images, and drug discovery.

6. **Finance:** AI is used in fraud detection, algorithmic trading, and credit scoring.

7. **Customer Service:** Chatbots and virtual agents increasingly handle customer inquiries.

8. **Language Translation:** AI-powered translation services have significantly improved recently.

Future Possibilities:

1. **Personalized Education:** AI could eventually provide individualised learning experiences, adapting to each

student's needs and learning style.

2. **Advanced Healthcare:** AI might enable early disease detection, personalised treatment plans, and even AI-assisted surgery.

3. **Smart Cities:** AI could optimise urban systems, from traffic flow to energy usage, creating more efficient and livable cities.

4. **Enhanced Creativity:** AI could become a powerful tool for artists, musicians, and writers, augmenting human creativity in new ways.

5. **Scientific Discovery:** AI might accelerate scientific research, helping solve complex problems in climate science and molecular biology.

6. **Augmented Reality:** AI could power more sophisticated AR experiences, blending digital information seamlessly with the physical world.

7. **Advanced Robotics:** More sophisticated AI could lead to robots capable of complex tasks in various environments, from homes to factories to disaster zones.

As AI becomes more pervasive, important questions arise: How do we ensure that AI systems respect privacy and individual autonomy? How might widespread AI affect employment and economic structures? And how do we maintain human agency and decision-making in a world increasingly mediated by AI?

4. The Ethics of AI: Navigating Uncharted Territory

As AI systems become more powerful and pervasive, they raise ethical concerns that society must grapple with. These issues touch on fundamental questions of fairness, privacy, accountability, and the very nature of human-machine interaction.

Bias and Fairness: AI systems can inadvertently perpetuate or amplify societal biases in training data. For example, facial recognition systems have shown lower accuracy rates for women and people of colour. Ensuring fairness in AI systems is crucial but complex, involving defining and measuring fairness across different contexts.

Privacy: AI's ability to process vast amounts of data raises significant privacy concerns. From facial recognition in public spaces to analysing online behaviour, AI technologies can enable unprecedented surveillance and data collection levels. Balancing the benefits of data-driven AI with individual privacy rights is a key challenge.

Transparency and Explainability: Many advanced AI systems, particularly those using deep learning, operate as "black boxes," making decisions in ways that are not easily interpretable by humans. This lack of transparency raises issues of accountability and trust, especially in high-stakes applications like healthcare or criminal justice.

Accountability: When AI systems make mistakes or cause harm, questions of liability and responsibility arise. Should the developers, the users, or the AI system be held accountable? As AI systems become more autonomous, these questions become increasingly complex.

Job Displacement: While AI has the potential to create new jobs, it also threatens to automate many existing roles. Managing this transition to minimise economic disruption and ensure fair distribution of AI benefits is a significant ethical and policy challenge.

Autonomy and Human Agency: As AI systems take on more decision-making roles, humans risk becoming overly reliant on or submissive to AI recommendations. Maintaining meaningful human agency in an AI-assisted world is crucial.

The weaponisation of AI: The potential use of AI in warfare, from autonomous weapons to AI-enhanced cyberattacks, raises serious ethical concerns about the future of conflict and human control over lethal decisions.

Existential Risk: While largely theoretical, the potential development of artificial general intelligence (AGI) or superintelligent AI raises profound questions about humanity's long-term future and survival.

<u>To address these ethical challenges, various approaches have been proposed:</u>

1. **Ethics by Design:** Incorporating ethical considerations into the development process of AI systems from the outset.

2. **Regulatory Frameworks:** Developing laws and regulations to govern the development and use of AI technologies.

3. **Ethics Boards:** Establishing independent bodies to provide ethical oversight for AI projects.

4. **Ethical AI Education:** Integrating ethics into the training of AI developers and users.

5. **Global Cooperation:** Fostering international collaboration to address the global implications of AI.

As we navigate these ethical challenges, key questions emerge: How do we align AI systems with human values when these values themselves can be diverse and conflicting? How do we balance innovation with caution in AI development? And how might our ethical frameworks need to evolve to address the unique challenges AI poses?

5. AI and the Future of Work

One of the most significant and contentious aspects of the AI revolution is its impact on the job market and the nature of work. While AI promises to increase productivity and create new opportunities, it also threatens to displace many existing jobs and radically reshape the employment landscape.

Job Displacement: Many routine and predictable tasks are at risk of automation. This includes manual labour and cognitive functions in data analysis, customer service, and creative fields. Economists and technologists are debating the pace and extent of this displacement.

New Job Creation: At the same time, AI is expected to create new jobs, many of which may not yet exist. These could include AI trainers, ethicists, and specialists in human-AI interaction. The challenge is to ensure that job creation keeps pace with displacement and that workers can transition to these new roles.

Changing Skill Requirements: As AI takes over routine tasks, human workers may need to focus more on skills that AI currently struggles with, such as complex problem-solving, creativity, emotional intelligence, and interpersonal skills. This shift will require significant changes in education and training systems.

Hybrid AI-Human Workflows: Many experts envision a future where AI augments human capabilities rather than simply replacing human workers. This could lead to new models of collaboration between humans and AI systems.

Gig Economy and Freelancing: AI could further grow the gig economy by making matching workers with short-term tasks easier. This trend raises questions about job security, benefits, and worker protections.

Income Inequality: There are concerns that AI could exacerbate income inequality by disproportionately benefiting those with the skills to work with AI systems or those with AI technologies.

Universal Basic Income: Some propose UBI as a potential solution to AI-driven job displacement, arguing that it could provide a safety net as the job market evolves.

Redefining Work and Value: As AI takes over more tasks, society may need to reconsider how we define work and value human contributions. This could lead to reevaluating unpaid work, such as caregiving, or a shift towards valuing uniquely human qualities.

As we consider the future of work in an AI-driven world, key questions arise: How can we ensure a just transition for workers displaced by AI? How might our education systems need to evolve to prepare people for this new reality? And how do we balance the economic benefits of AI automation with the social and psychological benefits of work?

6. AI and Creativity: Collaboration or Competition?

The relationship between AI and human creativity is complex and evolving. As AI systems become more sophisticated in areas traditionally seen as uniquely human—such as art, music, and writing—questions arise about the nature of creativity itself and the future role of human artists.

AI in the Creative Process:

1. Generation: AI can generate original content, from visual art to music to written text. Systems like DALL-E for image creation and GPT-3 for text generation have produced impressive results.

2. Augmentation: AI tools can help human creators by offering suggestions, automating routine tasks, or providing new ways to manipulate and explore creative materials.

3. Analysis: AI can analyse vast amounts of creative work, potentially uncovering patterns and insights that could inform new creations.

Implications for Human Creativity:

1. New Tools: AI offers artists powerful new tools for expression, potentially expanding the boundaries of what is creatively possible.

2. Democratization: AI could make certain forms of creation more accessible to those without traditional training.

3. Collaboration: Human-AI creative collaborations could lead to entirely new forms of art and expression.

4. Competition: There are concerns that AI-generated content could compete with human creators, potentially affecting livelihoods in creative industries.

5. Redefinition: As AI takes on more creative tasks, it may prompt a redefinition of what we consider uniquely human creativity.

Philosophical Questions:

1. Authorship: Who owns the rights to AI-generated or AI-assisted creative works?

2. Authenticity: How do we value AI-generated art compared to human-created art? Does the process matter as much as the final product?

3. Creativity vs. Generation: Is AI creative or generating content based on existing patterns? How do we define creativity in an age of AI?

4. Human Expression: If AI can create compelling art, what does this mean for art as a form of human expression and communication?

As AI develops in creative domains, key questions emerge: How can we harness AI to enhance rather than replace human creativity? How might our understanding and appreciation of art evolve in an era of AI-generated content? And what uniquely human elements of the creative process should we strive to preserve?

7. AI and Consciousness: The Final Frontier

As AI systems become more sophisticated, questions about machine consciousness and the nature of intelligence itself come to the forefront. While current AI is far from achieving consciousness, the possibility of conscious AI in the future raises profound philosophical and ethical questions.

Understanding Consciousness:

1. Philosopher David Chalmers used the term "the hard problem of consciousness" to describe the challenge of explaining how and why we have qualia, or subjective, conscious experiences.

2. Theories of Consciousness: Various theories attempt to explain consciousness, from neuroscientific approaches to philosophical concepts like panpsychism.

3. Measuring Consciousness: Debates continue about determining whether a being (human, animal, or artificial) is conscious.

AI and Consciousness:

<u>1. Weak AI vs. Strong AI:</u> Current AI (weak AI) is not conscious and operates on narrow, specific tasks. Strong AI, which would have human-like general intelligence, remains theoretical.

<u>2. Artificial General Intelligence (AGI):</u> The development of AGI, while still hypothetical, could bring us closer to questions of machine consciousness.

<u>3. Consciousness as Emergent:</u> Some theorise that consciousness could emerge in sufficiently complex AI systems, even if not explicitly programmed.

<u>Ethical Implications:</u>

<u>1. Moral Status:</u> If AI becomes conscious, what moral status should we accord it? Would it have rights?

<u>2. Treatment of AI:</u> How should we treat potentially conscious AI systems? This question becomes particularly pertinent in the context of AI used in social or emotional roles.

<u>3. AI Suffering:</u> If AI can be conscious, can it suffer? This could have significant implications for how we develop and use AI systems.

<u>Philosophical Questions:</u>

<u>1. Nature of Intelligence:</u> Does consciousness require human-like intelligence, or could there be radically different forms of conscious intelligence?

<u>2. Simulation and Reality:</u> If we create conscious AI, how would this impact our understanding of our consciousness and reality?

<u>3. Upload of Consciousness:</u> Some speculate about the possibility of uploading human consciousness into artificial systems. This raises questions about identity, continuity of

self, and the nature of human existence.

<u>Scientific Challenges:</u>

1. <u>Defining Consciousness:</u> Without a clear, agreed-upon definition of consciousness, creating or recognising it in AI systems remains challenging.

2. <u>Testing for Consciousness:</u> Developing reliable tests for machine consciousness is an open problem in philosophy and computer science.

3. <u>Ethical Experimentation:</u> Research into machine consciousness raises ethical questions about the potential creation of conscious entities for study.

While we consider the possibility of conscious AI, key questions emerge: How would the development of conscious AI change our understanding of consciousness itself? What ethical frameworks would we need to develop for potentially conscious machines? And how might the pursuit of machine consciousness illuminate our understanding of human consciousness?

8. AI and Religion: Ancient Wisdom Meets Cutting-Edge Technology

The development of AI raises intriguing questions when viewed through the lens of religious and spiritual traditions. While most sacred texts don't directly address AI, many religious concepts and ethical frameworks can provide valuable perspectives on the challenges posed by this technology.

<u>AI in Religious Contexts:</u>

1. <u>Creation and Creativity:</u> Many religions view the act of creation as a divine attribute. How does the creation of

intelligent machines align with or challenge these beliefs?

2. <u>Soul and Consciousness:</u> Religious concepts of the soul or spirit raise questions about the potential for machine consciousness and the uniqueness of human consciousness.

3. <u>Free Will:</u> Whether AI can have free will intersect with long-standing religious debates about determinism and human agency.

4. <u>Moral Status:</u> Religious teachings about the sanctity of life and the moral status of different beings could inform debates about the ethical treatment of advanced AI.

Biblical Perspectives:

1. **Stewardship:** The biblical concept of humans as stewards of creation (Genesis 1:28) could be interpreted as a call for responsible AI development and use.

   Further, God blessed them and said to them: "Be fruitful and become many, fill the earth and subdue it, and have in subjection the fish of the sea and the flying creatures of the heavens and every living creature that is moving on the earth."

Could AI assist in monitoring our planet and the creatures of the earth instead of facilitating its destruction?

2. **Wisdom and Discernment:** Proverbs' emphasis on wisdom and discernment (e.g., Proverbs 4:7) could guide ethical decision-making in AI development.

   "Wisdom is the most important thing, so acquire wisdom,
   And with all you acquire, acquire understanding."

Could increasing knowledge and understanding about AI prevent its senseless and undiscerning use by a few, affecting the lives of many?

3. **Humility:** Biblical warnings against human hubris (e.g., the Tower of Babel story) might caution against overconfidence in our ability to control advanced AI.

4. **Love and Compassion:** The Christian emphasis on love (e.g., 1 Corinthians 13) could inform discussions about maintaining human empathy and compassion in an AI-driven world.

"Love is patient and kind. Love is not jealous. It does not brag, does not get puffed up, does not behave indecently, does not look for its own interests, does not become provoked. It does not keep account of the injury. It does not rejoice over unrighteousness but rejoices with the truth. It bears all things, believes all things, hopes all things, endures all things. Love never fails. But if there are gifts of prophecy, they will be done away with; if there are tongues, they will cease; if there is knowledge, it will be done away with. For we have partial knowledge and we prophesy partially, but when what is complete comes, what is partial will be done away with."

Could AI be developed without concealed agenda?

5. **Image of God:** The concept of humans being created in God's image (Genesis 1:27) raises questions about the uniqueness of human intelligence and creativity in the face of advanced AI.

"And God went on to create the man in his image, in God's image he created him; male and female he created them."

AI in Other Religious Traditions:

1. **Buddhism:** Buddhist concepts of non-self and interdependence could offer interesting perspectives on machine consciousness and the nature of intelligence.

2. **Hinduism:** Hindu philosophy's concept of Maya (illusion) and debates about the nature of consciousness could

contribute to discussions about AI and reality.

3. **Islam:** Islamic teachings on knowledge and ethical use of technology could guide Muslim approaches to AI development and deployment.

4. **Judaism:** The Jewish tradition of ethical debate and interpretation could provide a model for grappling with the complex moral questions raised by AI.

Practical Intersections:

1. **Religious AI:** Some have explored the creation of AI systems that perform religious functions, such as chatbots that offer spiritual advice or AI systems that analyse religious texts.

2. **Ethical AI Development:** Religious, ethical frameworks could inform the development of AI ethics guidelines and policies.

3. **Transhumanism:** Some view the development of AI and human augmentation technologies as a path to transcendence, using a quasi-religious lens.

4. **Interfaith Dialogue:** AI's challenges could catalyse interfaith dialogue and cooperation on shared ethical concerns.

Challenges and Questions:

1. **Anthropomorphism:** How do religious tendencies to anthropomorphise the divine influence our perception and treatment of AI?

2. **Technological Determinism:** How do we balance religious perspectives on divine providence with the rapid advancement of AI technologies?

3. **Existential Questions:** How might the development of AGI or superintelligent AI challenge or reshape religious understandings of human uniqueness and purpose?

4. **Ethical Frameworks:** How can religious and ethical traditions be applied to novel situations created by AI not envisioned by ancient texts or traditions?

While we consider the intersection of AI and religion, key questions emerge: How can ancient wisdom traditions inform our approach to cutting-edge technology? How might the development of AI challenge or reshape religious beliefs and practices? And how can diverse religious perspectives contribute to global discussions about the ethical development and use of AI?

9. AI and Education: Reshaping Learning in the Digital Age

The integration of AI into education has the potential to transform how we teach and learn dramatically. From personalised learning experiences to administrative efficiencies, AI offers exciting possibilities and significant challenges for educational systems worldwide.

<u>Current and Potential Applications:</u>

1. **Personalized Learning:** AI can analyse individual student performance and learning styles to tailor educational content and pacing.

2. **Intelligent Tutoring Systems:** AI-powered tutors can provide one-on-one support, answering questions and offering real-time explanations.

3. **Automated Grading:** AI can assist in grading objective assessments and even provide initial feedback on essays and other written work.

4. **Predictive Analytics:** AI can help identify students at risk of falling behind or dropping out, allowing for early intervention.

5. **Administrative Tasks:** AI can streamline administrative processes, freeing up time for educators to focus on teaching.

6. **Adaptive Assessments:** AI-powered tests can adjust difficulty based on student performance, providing more accurate evaluations.

7. **Language Learning:** AI language models can provide immersive language practice and instant feedback.

8. **Accessibility:** AI can help make educational content more accessible to students with disabilities through technologies like real-time captioning or text-to-speech.

Potential Benefits:

1. **Individualization:** AI can help address the long-standing challenge of providing individualised education at scale.

2. **24/7 Access:** AI tutors and learning systems can provide round-the-clock educational support.

3. **Data-Driven Insights:** AI can offer detailed analytics on student performance and learning patterns, which can inform educational strategies.

4. **Global Reach:** AI-powered online learning platforms can extend educational opportunities to underserved areas.

Challenges and Concerns:

1. **Digital Divide:** The reliance on AI in education could exacerbate existing inequalities in access to technology and high-quality education.

2. **Privacy:** The collection and use of student data raise

significant privacy concerns.

3. **Human Touch:** There's a risk of losing education's critical social and emotional aspects from human-to-human interaction.

4. **Teacher Role:** The integration of AI will likely require a shift in the role of teachers, necessitating new skills and approaches.

5. **Critical Thinking:** While AI can efficiently convey information, fostering critical thinking and creativity may require human guidance.

6. **Bias:** AI systems may perpetuate or amplify biases in their training data or design.

Ethical Considerations:

1. **Transparency:** How can we ensure that AI-driven educational decisions are transparent and explainable to students, parents, and educators?

2. **Autonomy:** How do we balance the benefits of AI-driven personalisation with student and teacher autonomy in the learning process?

3. **Holistic Development:** How can we ensure that AI in education supports academic learning and social, emotional, and ethical development?

Future Directions:

1. **AI Literacy:** As AI technology becomes more pervasive, educating students about AI will likely become essential to the curriculum.

2. **Hybrid Models:** The future of education may involve

a careful balance of AI-assisted and traditional human-led instruction.

3. **Lifelong Learning:** AI could support more effective continuous, lifelong learning models to help individuals adapt to a rapidly changing job market.

While we consider AI's role in reshaping education, key questions emerge: How can we harness AI's power to provide high-quality, personalised education while preserving the essential human elements of teaching and learning? How do we prepare students for a world where AI is ubiquitous? And how can we ensure that the integration of AI in education promotes equity and access rather than exacerbating existing disparities?

10. AI and Healthcare: Revolutionizing Patient Care

Artificial Intelligence has the potential to dramatically transform healthcare, offering new tools for diagnosis, treatment, and patient care. From analysing medical images to predicting disease outbreaks, AI is already making significant impacts in the medical field.

Current and Potential Applications:

1. **Diagnosis:** AI can analyse medical images (X-rays, MRIs, CT scans) to detect abnormalities, often with accuracy rivalling or surpassing human experts.

2. **Drug Discovery:** AI can accelerate the identification of potential new drugs and predict their effects.

3. **Personalized Medicine:** AI can help tailor treatments to individual patients by analysing vast amounts of patient data.

4. **Predictive Analytics:** AI can identify certain conditions in high-risk patients, enabling preventive interventions.

5. **Robot-Assisted Surgery:** AI-powered surgical robots can assist in complex procedures, enhancing precision and reducing invasiveness.

6. **Virtual Nursing Assistants:** AI chatbots can provide essential patient monitoring and answer routine medical questions.

7. **Administrative Tasks:** AI can streamline hospital workflows, manage electronic health records, and handle billing and insurance claims.

8. **Epidemic Outbreak Prediction:** AI can analyse patterns in data to predict and track disease outbreaks.

<u>Potential Benefits:</u>

1. **Improved Accuracy:** In many diagnostic tasks, AI has shown the ability to reduce error rates.

2. **Efficiency:** AI can quickly process vast amounts of medical data, potentially speeding up diagnosis and treatment planning.

3. **Accessibility:** AI-powered telemedicine can extend healthcare services to underserved areas.

4. **Cost Reduction:** Automation of routine tasks and improved efficiency could help reduce healthcare costs.

5. **24/7 Monitoring:** AI systems can provide continuous patient monitoring, alerting healthcare providers to potential issues in real time.

<u>Challenges and Concerns:</u>

1. **Data Privacy:** Using personal health data raises significant privacy concerns.

2. **Bias:** AI systems may perpetuate or amplify biases in their training data, potentially leading to disparities in care.

3. **Liability:** When AI systems are involved in medical decisions, questions of liability in case of errors become complex.

4. **Human Touch:** There's a risk of losing the empathy and personal connection crucial in healthcare.

5. **Over-reliance:** There's a danger that healthcare providers might over-rely on AI recommendations, potentially overlooking essential factors.

6. **Integration:** Incorporating AI systems into healthcare workflows and infrastructure poses significant challenges.

<u>Ethical Considerations:</u>

1. **Informed Consent:** How do we ensure patients understand and consent to using AI in their care?

2. **Equity:** How can we ensure that AI-driven healthcare benefits all populations equally?

3. **Human Oversight:** What's the appropriate balance between AI autonomy and human oversight in medical decision-making?

4. **Transparency:** How can we make AI systems in healthcare more explainable and transparent?

<u>Future Directions:</u>

1. **AI-Human Collaboration:** The future likely involves close collaboration between AI systems and human healthcare providers, each leveraging their unique strengths.

2. **Preventive Care:** AI could enable a shift towards more

preventive and predictive healthcare models.

3. **Personalized Health Monitoring:** AI-powered wearables and home devices could provide continuous health monitoring and early warning systems.

4. **Global Health:** AI could be crucial in addressing global health challenges, from predicting pandemics to optimising resource allocation in low-resource settings.

As we consider AI's role in healthcare, key questions emerge: How can we integrate AI into healthcare systems to enhance rather than replace the human elements of care? How do we balance the potential benefits of AI in healthcare with concerns about privacy and equity? How might AI change our fundamental approaches to health and medicine?

11. AI and Environmental Sustainability: A Double-Edged Sword

Artificial Intelligence has emerged as a powerful tool for addressing environmental challenges. It offers new ways to monitor, predict, and mitigate human impacts on the planet. However, the technology itself has significant ecological implications.

<u>Positive Applications:</u>

1. **Climate Modeling:** AI can process vast amounts of climate data to create more accurate climate change models and predictions.

2. **Energy Efficiency:** AI can optimise energy use in buildings, transportation systems, and industrial processes.

3. **Renewable Energy:** AI can improve the efficiency of renewable energy systems, from predicting wind patterns for wind farms to optimising solar panel placement.

4. **Wildlife Conservation:** AI-powered image recognition can track and monitor wildlife populations.

5. **Waste Management:** AI can improve recycling processes and optimise waste collection routes.

6. **Agriculture:** AI can help optimise crop yields while minimising water use and pesticide application.

7. **Environmental Monitoring:** AI can analyse satellite imagery and sensor data to detect deforestation, pollution, and other environmental changes.

8. **Disaster Prediction and Response:** AI can help predict natural disasters and optimise emergency response efforts.

Challenges and Concerns:

1. **Energy Consumption:** Training and running large AI models requires significant computational power, which can have a substantial carbon footprint.

2. **E-Waste:** The rapid advancement of AI hardware contributes to electronic waste.

3. **Resource Extraction:** The production of AI hardware requires rare earth elements and other materials, the extraction of which can have significant environmental impacts.

4. **Rebound Effects:** Efficiency gains from AI could lead to increased consumption, potentially offsetting environmental benefits.

5. **Bias in Environmental Data:** AI systems may perpetuate or amplify environmental data collection and analysis biases.

Ethical Considerations:

1. **Balancing Priorities**: How do we balance AI's potential environmental benefits against its ecological costs?

2. **Global Equity:** How can we ensure that AI-driven environmental solutions benefit all populations, not just wealthy nations?

3. **Transparency:** How can we make AI-driven environmental decisions more transparent and accountable?

4. **Long-term Impacts:** How do we account for AI systems' long-term and potentially unforeseen environmental impacts?

<u>Future Directions:</u>

1. **Green AI:** Developing more energy-efficient AI algorithms and hardware.

2. **AI for Circular Economy:** Using AI to design and implement more effective circular economy systems.

3. **Environmental AI Ethics:** Incorporating environmental considerations into AI ethics frameworks.

4. **AI-Powered Environmental Education:** Using AI to create more engaging and personalised environmental education tools.

As we consider AI's role in environmental sustainability, key questions emerge: How can we harness AI's power to address ecological challenges while minimising its environmental impact? How might AI change our approaches to environmental management and conservation? How can we ensure that AI-driven environmental solutions are fair and globally beneficial?

12. The Geopolitics of AI: A New Arena for Global

Competition

The development and control of AI technologies have become significant factors in global politics and economics. Nations are vying for leadership in what many see as a critical domain for future power and prosperity.

<u>Key Areas of Competition:</u>

1. **Research and Development:** Countries invest heavily in AI R&D to gain a technological edge.

2. **Talent Acquisition:** Global competition exists to attract and retain top AI researchers and engineers.

3. **Data Control:** Access to large datasets is crucial for AI development, making data a valuable geopolitical resource.

4. **AI Ethics and Governance:** Nations compete to set global standards and norms for AI development and use.

5. **Military Applications:** AI is seen as a game-changer in military technology, sparking a new arms race.

6. **Economic Impact:** AI's potential to drive economic growth is key to global economic competition.

<u>Major Players:</u>

1. **United States:** Leader in AI research and home to many of the world's top AI companies.

2. **China:** Rapidly advancing in AI, with strong government support and access to vast amounts of data.

3. **European Union:** Focused on ethical AI development and digital sovereignty.

4. **Russia:** Emphasizing military applications of AI.

5. Other nations like Israel, Canada, and South Korea are significant players in specific AI domains.

Challenges and Concerns:

1. **AI Nationalism:** The trend towards treating AI as a national asset could hinder global cooperation on AI challenges.

2. **Digital Colonialism:** Concerns that AI could enable new forms of economic and cultural domination by technologically advanced nations.

3. **Surveillance and Control:** AI's potential to enhance state surveillance and social control raises human rights concerns.

4. **Autonomous Weapons:** Developing AI-powered autonomous weapons systems is a central ethical and security concern.

5. **Brain Drain:** The concentration of AI talent in a few countries could exacerbate global inequalities.

Ethical Considerations:

1. **Global Equity:** How can we ensure that AI's benefits are distributed globally, not just to a few powerful nations?

2. **AI for Good:** How can international cooperation on AI be fostered to address global challenges like climate change and poverty?

3. **Human Rights:** How do we protect human rights and civil liberties in the face of AI-enhanced state power?

4. **Accountability:** How can we create global governance systems and accountability for AI development and use?

Future Directions:

1. **International AI Treaties:** There are calls for international agreements to govern AI development and use, similar to nuclear non-proliferation treaties.

2. **AI Diplomacy:** AI issues will likely become increasingly important in international diplomacy and negotiation.

3. **Global AI Ethics Framework:** Efforts to develop globally accepted ethical guidelines for AI.

4. **AI for Sustainable Development:** Initiatives to harness AI for achieving the UN Sustainable Development Goals.

As we consider the geopolitics of AI, key questions emerge: How can we foster international cooperation on AI development while managing competition? How might AI reshape the global balance of power? And how can we ensure that the global race for AI supremacy doesn't compromise ethical standards or exacerbate global inequalities?

13. Conclusion: Charting a Course Through the AI Revolution

As we conclude our exploration of AI's promise and peril, we find ourselves at a critical juncture in human history. Artificial Intelligence represents one of the most influential and transformative technologies ever developed, potentially reshaping nearly every aspect of our lives and societies.

The promise of AI is immense. From revolutionising healthcare and education to addressing climate change and enhancing scientific discovery, AI offers tools that could help us solve some of humanity's most pressing challenges. It has the potential to augment human capabilities, free us from routine tasks, and open new frontiers of creativity and innovation.

Yet the perils are equally significant. The potential for job displacement, the exacerbation of existing inequalities, the risks to privacy and autonomy, and the profound ethical quandaries raised by increasingly autonomous systems all demand our careful attention. The possibility, however remote, of artificial general intelligence or superintelligence presents existential questions about humanity's future.

Navigating this landscape requires a delicate balance:

1. **Innovation and Caution:** We must foster AI innovation while proceeding with appropriate caution and foresight.

2. **Benefit and Risk:** We must maximise AI's benefits while mitigating risks and potential negative impacts.

3. **Global Competition and Cooperation:** While AI has become an arena for national competition, global cooperation is essential to address its worldwide implications.

4. **Efficiency and Humanity:** As we harness AI to increase efficiency and productivity, we must remember uniquely human values and qualities.

5. **Present and Future:** We must address immediate AI-related challenges while preparing for longer-term, potentially transformative developments.

Moving forward, several key principles might guide our approach to AI:

1. **Ethical Framework:** Developing and adhering to robust ethical AI development and deployment guidelines.

2. **Inclusivity:** Ensuring that the development and benefits of AI are inclusive, representing diverse perspectives and benefiting all of humanity.

3. **Transparency and Accountability:** Promoting transparency in AI systems and clear lines of accountability

for their impacts.

4. **Human-Centered Design:** Keeping human needs, rights, and values at the centre of AI development.

5. **Interdisciplinary Approach:** Recognizing that AI challenges cut across technical, social, ethical, and philosophical domains, requiring diverse expertise.

6. **Lifelong Learning:** Fostering a culture of continuous learning to help individuals adapt to AI-driven changes.

7. **Global Governance:** Working towards international frameworks for AI governance that can address its global implications.

As we chart our course through the AI revolution, we must also remain humble in the face of uncertainty. The full implications of AI are still unfolding, and our ability to predict its long-term impacts is limited. This uncertainty calls for adaptability, ongoing dialogue, and a willingness to revise our approaches as we learn more.

Moreover, as we grapple with AI's profound questions, we can reflect deeply on what it means to be human. AI challenges us to articulate the qualities we value most in human intelligence and consciousness. It prompts us to consider the nature of creativity, emotion, and ethical reasoning. In this way, the development of AI becomes not just a technological endeavour but a philosophical and reflective one.

We must also consider the narrative we craft around AI. While awareness of the risks is crucial, an overly dystopian view could lead to paralysing fear or restrictive policies that stifle beneficial innovation. Conversely, an uncritically utopian view could lead to complacency about real risks. We need a balanced narrative acknowledging AI's transformative potential and serious challenges.

Education will play a crucial role in the future of AI. We must promote widespread AI literacy and help people understand AI systems' capabilities and limitations. This education should extend beyond technical knowledge to include AI's ethical, social, and philosophical dimensions.

Looking to the future, AI will be a defining feature of the 21st century and beyond. How we develop and deploy this technology will shape the trajectory of human civilisation. The choices we make now will have profound implications for future generations.

We might draw wisdom from various sources, including ancient philosophical and spiritual traditions, to address this challenge. Many of these traditions emphasise understanding, compassion, and the interconnectedness of all things, which could provide valuable guidance as we navigate the complexities of AI.

Ultimately, the story of AI is our story. It's a testament to human ingenuity and our quest to understand and augment our intelligence. But it also reflects our fears, ethical dilemmas, and ongoing struggle to use our creations wisely and for the greater good.

As we stand on the brink of this new era, we are called upon to exercise our uniquely human capacities for foresight, ethical reasoning, and collective action. The future of AI is not predetermined; it will be shaped by our choices and the values we prioritise.

In conclusion, the AI revolution presents us with extraordinary opportunities and daunting challenges. Bearing in mind that AI is a programmed intelligence written by human AI output can be biased or make mistakes, by approaching these with wisdom, ethical commitment, and a spirit of global cooperation, we can work towards a future where AI serves as a powerful tool for human flourishing and the betterment of our world. The promise and peril of AI are not set in stone – they are in our hands to shape. Let us embrace this responsibility with the gravity it deserves and the hope it inspires.

CHAPTER 6: BIG PHARMA: HEALING OR HUBRIS?

1. Introduction: The Pharmaceutical Industry at a Crossroads

The pharmaceutical industry, colloquially known as "Big Pharma," stands at the intersection of some of the most critical issues of our time: public health, scientific innovation, economic power, and ethical responsibility. This industry, which has brought life-saving medications to millions and generated immense wealth, is also the subject of intense scrutiny and criticism.

In this chapter, we will explore the complex landscape of the pharmaceutical industry, examining its achievements, challenges, and the ethical dilemmas it faces. We'll delve into the industry's business models, research practices, marketing strategies, and global impact. We'll consider how the profit motive in pharmaceutical research and development interacts with the ethical imperative to improve human health.

Our exploration will be critical and nuanced. We will recognise pharmaceuticals' vital role in modern healthcare and address the serious concerns raised about industry practices. We will draw on insights from medicine, economics, ethics, and public policy to comprehensively view this crucial sector.

As we navigate this complex topic, we will also consider perspectives from various ethical frameworks, including those in ancient wisdom traditions and religious texts. These timeless insights may offer valuable guidance as we grapple with balancing profit, innovation, and public health in the 21st century.

By understanding the mechanisms, motivations, and changes of the pharmaceutical industry, we can work towards a future where the immense power of modern medicine is harnessed more effectively and ethically for the benefit of all humanity.

2. The Evolution of the Pharmaceutical Industry

To understand the pharmaceutical industry's current state, it's crucial to trace its historical development. Although the modern sector has its roots in the 19th century, its transformation into the global powerhouse we know today is primarily a product of the 20th century.

Early Beginnings:

19th century: The isolation of active compounds from plants and the development of synthetic dyes, which led to early drug discoveries, laid the foundations of the modern pharmaceutical industry.

- **Late 19th/early 20th century:** Companies like Merck, Pfizer, and Bayer, originally chemical or dye manufacturers, began producing medicines.

The Golden Age of Drug Discovery:

- **1930s-1960s:** This period saw the discovery and mass production of antibiotics, starting with penicillin. It marked a medical revolution and established the pharmaceutical industry as a significant economic force.

- **Post-World War II:** Rapid advances in scientific understanding led to the development of many new classes of drugs, including psychotropic medications, oral contraceptives, and treatments for chronic diseases.

The Rise of Regulation:

- 1962: The Kefauver-Harris Amendment in the U.S. required drug manufacturers to provide proof of effectiveness and safety before approval, significantly impacting drug development processes and costs.

- 1970s-1980s: Increased regulation led to longer drug development times and higher costs, shaping the industry's current high-risk, high-reward model.

The Era of Blockbuster Drugs:

From the 1980s to the 2000s, the industry focused on developing "blockbuster" drugs—medications with annual sales of over $1 billion. This model drove unprecedented profits and shaped research priorities.

- Patents became increasingly crucial, with companies racing to develop patentable modifications of existing drugs.

Globalisation and Consolidation:

- Late 20th/early 21st century: The industry became increasingly global, with companies expanding into emerging markets.

- A wave of mergers and acquisitions led to the formation of a handful of substantial multinational corporations.

The Biotech Revolution:

- 1980s onwards: The rise of biotechnology opened new avenues for drug discovery, leading to the development of biological drugs and personalised medicine approaches.

- Many large pharmaceutical companies began acquiring or partnering with smaller biotech firms.

<u>Current Challenges:</u>

- Patent cliffs: As patents on blockbuster drugs expire, companies face revenue losses to generic competition.

- Declining R&D productivity: Despite increased spending, the rate of new drug approvals has yet to keep pace.

- Pricing controversies: High drug prices have led to public backlash and calls for reform.

- Shift towards rare diseases and personalised medicine: Companies increasingly focus on treatments for smaller patient populations.

This historical trajectory raises essential questions: How has the industry's evolution shaped its current priorities and practices? Has the increasing commercialisation of drug development enhanced or hindered the industry's ability to address global health needs? And how might the industry's past inform potential future directions?

3. The Business of Pharmaceuticals: Profit and Public Health

The pharmaceutical industry operates at a unique intersection of science, healthcare, and business. Its business model, which relies on high-risk, high-reward drug development, has significant implications for public health and corporate profits.

Key Components of the Pharmaceutical Business Model:

1. **Research and Development (R&D):**

- Long, costly process: Developing a new drug typically takes 10-15 years and costs over $1 billion.

- High failure rate: Only about 1 in 10 drugs that enter clinical trials ultimately get approved.

- Focus on patentable innovations: The potential for patent protection drives research directions.

2. **Patents and Market Exclusivity:**

Patents typically last 20 years from filing, but practical patent life is often shorter due to the time it takes for development and approval.

- Market exclusivity allows companies to set high prices to recoup R&D costs and generate profits.

3. **Marketing and Sales:**

- Significant resources are devoted to marketing drugs to healthcare providers and, in some countries, directly to consumers.

- Sales representatives play a crucial role in promoting drugs to doctors.

4. **Pricing Strategies:**

- Prices are often highest in the U.S., with fewer price controls.

- Differential pricing strategies are used in different markets.

- High prices are justified by companies as necessary to fund future R&D, but this is often contested.

5. **Mergers and Acquisitions:**

- Large companies often acquire smaller firms with promising drug candidates to bolster their pipelines.

6. **Generics and Biosimilars:**

- After patent expiration, companies compete with lower-priced generic drugs or biosimilars.

Implications of this Business Model:

1. **Innovation vs. Imitation:** The current model incentivises incremental improvements to existing drugs (so-called "me-too" drugs) that can be patented, potentially at the expense of more innovative but riskier research.

2. **Neglected Diseases:** Due to limited profit potential, diseases primarily affecting low-income populations often receive less research attention.

3. **Focus on Chronic Diseases:** Medications for chronic conditions that require long-term use are often prioritised over one-time treatments.

4. **Access Issues:** High drug prices can limit access, particularly in low- and middle-income countries and for uninsured or underinsured populations in wealthy countries.

5. **Research Bias:** The need to protect valuable intellectual property can lead to a lack of transparency in research.

6. **Regulatory Capture:** The industry's economic power can lead to outsized influence on drug regulation and health policy.

Ethical Considerations:

1. **Balancing Profit and Public Health:** How can the industry's

need for profitability be balanced with the imperative to address global health needs?

2. **Fair Pricing:** What constitutes a fair price for a drug, considering the need to incentivise innovation and ensure access?

3. **Research Priorities:** How should research priorities be set to serve public health needs best?

4. **Transparency:** How can greater transparency be encouraged without compromising legitimate business interests?

<u>Alternative Models:</u>

1. **Public-Private Partnerships:** Collaborations between industry, government, and non-profits to address neglected diseases or antibiotics development.

2. **Prize Funds:** Offering substantial monetary prizes for developing drugs for specific conditions, decoupling R&D costs from drug prices.

3. **Government-Funded Research:** Expanding public funding for drug discovery and development.

4. **Patent Pools:** Sharing patents to facilitate the development of new combination therapies, particularly for diseases affecting low-income countries.

As we consider the pharmaceutical business, key questions emerge: How can we create a system that harnesses the innovative potential of the private sector while ensuring that public health needs are met? Can we develop new models that align profit incentives with global health priorities? And how do we ensure that the pharmaceutical industry's immense resources are deployed in ways that maximise humanity's benefit?

4. Drug Development: From Lab to Market

Bringing a new drug to market is long, complex, and challenging. Understanding this process is crucial for addressing the high drug development costs and ethical issues that arise.

Stages of Drug Development:

1. **Basic Research and Drug Discovery:**

   - It often begins in academic or government labs, where disease mechanisms are studied, and potential drug targets are identified.

   - High-throughput screening of thousands of compounds to find promising candidates.

   - Increasing use of computer modelling and AI in drug discovery.

2. **Preclinical Studies:**

   - Testing in laboratory and animal models to assess safety and efficacy.

   - Optimization of drug candidates for stability, absorption, and other properties.

   - Preparation of data for regulatory submission to begin human trials.

3. **Clinical Trials:**

   - Phase I: Small trials in healthy volunteers to assess safety and dosing.

- Phase II: Larger trials in patients to evaluate efficacy and side effects.

- Phase III: Large-scale trials to confirm effectiveness, monitor side effects, and compare with current treatments.

4. Regulatory Review and Approval:

- Give all data to regulatory agencies (e.g., FDA in the U.S., EMA in Europe).

The review process can take 6-10 months or longer.

- Possible requirement for more studies.

5. Post-Market Surveillance:

- Ongoing monitoring of the drug's safety and effectiveness in the broader population.

- Sometimes includes Phase IV trials to study long-term effects or new indications.

Key Challenges in Drug Development:

1. **High Failure Rates:** Most drug candidates fail during development, often in late, expensive stages.

2. **Rising Costs:** The cost of bringing a new drug to market has increased dramatically, driven by more extensive and complex clinical trials, stricter regulatory requirements, and the increasing difficulty of finding novel and effective treatments.

3. **Long Timelines:** The process typically takes 10-15 years, affecting patent life and return on investment.

4. **Regulatory Hurdles:** Navigating complex and sometimes differing regulatory requirements across countries can be challenging and time-consuming.

5. **Recruitment for Clinical Trials:** Finding enough suitable participants for trials can be difficult, especially for rare diseases.

6. **Ethical Considerations in Human Testing:** Ensuring informed consent, managing risks to participants, and dealing with issues like placebo use in serious diseases.

Ethical Issues in Drug Development:

1. **Trial Design and Placebo Use:** This involves balancing the need for scientific rigour with the ethical imperative to provide treatment to all participants.

2. **Vulnerable Populations:** Adequate protections for vulnerable groups, including children, older people, and populations in developing countries, must be ensured in clinical trials.

3. **Publication Bias** is the tendency to publish positive results while suppressing negative ones, skewing the scientific record.

4. **Data Transparency:** Debates over how much trial data should be publicly available.

5. **Animal Testing:** Ethical concerns about using animals in preclinical studies must be balanced against the need to ensure human safety.

6. **Conflict of Interest:** When researchers have financial interests in the drugs they study, they must manage potential conflicts.

7. **Expanded Access:** Balancing requests for pre-approval access to experimental drugs with the need to complete controlled trials.

Emerging Trends and Potential Solutions:

1. **Adaptive Trial Designs:** These are more flexible trial designs that can adapt based on interim results, potentially speeding up the process.

2. **Biomarkers and Precision Medicine:** Genetic and other biomarkers can identify patients most likely to benefit from a treatment, potentially making trials more efficient.

3. **Real-World Evidence:** Incorporating data from electronic health records and other real-world sources to supplement traditional clinical trials.

4. **Patient-Centered Drug Development:** Increasing involvement of patients in trial design and outcome selection.

5. **Global Regulatory Harmonization:** Efforts to align regulatory requirements across countries to streamline the approval process.

6. **Artificial Intelligence:** Using AI to predict drug safety and efficacy, potentially reducing failure rates and costs.

As we consider the drug development process, key questions emerge: How can we streamline it without compromising safety? How do we ensure that the developed drugs address the most pressing health needs? How can we make the clinical trial process more ethical, efficient, and representative of diverse populations?

5. Marketing and Promotion: Informing or Influencing?

The marketing and promotion of pharmaceutical products play a crucial role in the industry's business model, but these practices have also been the source of significant controversy and ethical debate.

<u>Key Aspects of Pharmaceutical Marketing:</u>

1. **Direct-to-Consumer Advertising (DTCA):**

   - Legal in only a few countries, notably the U.S. and New Zealand.

   - Includes TV commercials, print ads, and online marketing.

   - Advocates argue it educates patients; critics say it leads to overmedication and higher healthcare costs.

2. **Marketing to Healthcare Providers:**

   - Sales representatives (often called "drug reps") visit doctors to promote products.

   - Sponsorship of continuing medical education events.

   - Provision of drug samples to doctors.

3. **Key Opinion Leaders (KOLs):**

   - Influential doctors and researchers often discuss drugs at conferences or write articles.

   - Raises concerns about potential bias and conflict of interest.

4. **Medical Journal Advertising and Publications:**

   - Ads in Medical Journals.

   - Publication of clinical trial results, sometimes with industry involvement in manuscript preparation.

5. **Digital Marketing:**

   - Increasing use of social media, online ads, and disease awareness websites.

   - Challenges in regulating online pharmaceutical marketing.

Ethical Concerns and Criticisms:

1. **Overmedicalization:** Concerns that marketing creates or exaggerates health concerns, leading to unnecessary drug use.

2. **Biased Information:** Critics argue that marketing often presents an overly optimistic view of drugs, downplaying risks and limitations.

3. **Influence on Prescribing Habits:** Studies suggest that marketing activities can influence doctors' prescribing decisions, potentially prioritising newer, more expensive drugs over equally effective alternatives.

4. **Ghostwriting:** The practice of pharmaceutical companies drafting articles published under academic authors' names.

5. **Off-label Promotion:** Illegal promotion of drugs for uses not approved by regulatory agencies has resulted in several high-profile legal cases.

6. **Disease Mongering:** Accusations that the industry promotes medicalising normal conditions to expand markets.

7. **Patient Group Funding:** Concerns about the influence of industry funding on patient advocacy groups.

Regulatory Landscape:

1. **Varying Global Regulations:** Marketing rules differ significantly between countries, creating challenges for global companies.

2. **FDA Oversight in the U.S.:** Strict rules on claims can be made in advertisements and requirements for a fair balance of risk and benefit information.

3. **Industry Self-regulation:** Many countries have industry

codes of practice, but their effectiveness is debated.

4. **Sunshine Acts:** Laws requiring disclosure of payments from pharmaceutical companies to healthcare providers.

Emerging Trends and Potential Solutions:

1. **Increased Transparency:** Companies are increasingly pressured to disclose all payments to healthcare providers and patient groups.

2. **Digital Ethics:** Development of ethical guidelines for pharmaceutical marketing in the digital age.

3. **Value-based Marketing is a** shift toward emphasising a drug's value regarding patient outcomes rather than just its features.

4. **Patient-centered Approaches:** Increasing focus on patient education and support programs rather than traditional promotional activities.

5. **Regulatory Technology:** Use AI and big data to monitor and enforce marketing regulations effectively.

Ethical Considerations:

1. **Right to Information:** Balancing the public's right to information about medical treatments with the need to protect against misleading claims.

2. **Doctor-Patient Relationship:** How does pharmaceutical marketing impact the trusted relationship between healthcare providers and patients?

3. **Health Literacy:** How can marketing contribute to improved health literacy rather than simply promoting specific products?

4. **Global Equity:** How do we address disparities in access to medical information and treatments between high- and low-income countries?

As we consider pharmaceutical marketing practices, key questions emerge: How can we ensure that marketing serves to educate and inform rather than increase sales? What role should the industry play in disseminating medical information? How can we create systems prioritising patient welfare over commercial interests while allowing legitimate business activities?

6. Pricing and Access: The Cost of Health

The pricing of pharmaceutical products is one of the industry's most contentious issues. High drug prices, particularly in the United States, have sparked intense debate about the balance between incentivising innovation and ensuring access to essential medicines.

<u>Key Factors Influencing Drug Pricing:</u>

1. **Research and Development Costs:** Companies justify high prices by citing the high costs and risks involved in drug development.

2. **Market Exclusivity:** Patent protection allows companies to set high prices during the exclusivity period.

3. **Value-based Pricing:** Some argue prices should reflect the value a drug provides in terms of health outcomes and quality of life improvements.

4. **Market Dynamics:** Prices can be influenced by competition, or lack thereof, in a particular therapeutic area.

5. **Regulatory Environment:** Different countries have varying levels of price controls and negotiation power.

6. **Manufacturing and Distribution Costs**: Though often smaller, these costs affect pricing.

7. **Profit Margins:** Pharmaceutical companies often have higher profit margins than other industries, which they argue is necessary to fund ongoing R&D and compensate for the high risks.

8. **Global Pricing Strategies:** Companies often use differential pricing across markets, charging higher prices in wealthy countries to subsidise lower prices in poorer nations.

<u>Challenges and Controversies:</u>

1. **High Prices in the U.S.:** Due to limited government price negotiation, the U.S. generally has the highest drug prices globally.

2. **Price Hikes on Existing Drugs:** Significant price increases on long-established drugs have attracted criticism and regulatory scrutiny.

3. **Orphan Drugs:** Extremely high prices for drugs treating rare diseases, justified by small patient populations but often controversial.

4. **Launch Prices:** The trend of increasingly high prices for newly launched drugs, especially in areas like oncology.

5. **Global Access Disparities:** Many patients in low—and middle-income countries need help affording or accessing essential medicines.

6. **Insurance and Out-of-Pocket Costs:** Even in wealthy countries, high drug prices can lead to significant out-of-pocket patient costs.

7. **Biosimilars and Generics:** Debates over the appropriate

balance between incentivising innovation and facilitating market competition.

Ethical Considerations:

1. **Right to Health:** How do we balance intellectual property rights with the human right to health and access to essential medicines?

2. **Fair Pricing:** What constitutes a fair price for a drug, considering the need to incentivise innovation and ensure access?

3. **Global Equity:** How can we ensure fair access to medicines globally without undermining incentives for innovation?

4. **Transparency:** Should pharmaceutical companies be required to disclose their costs and profit margins to justify their pricing?

5. **Societal Value:** How should the broader societal value of a drug (e.g., reduced hospitalisations and improved productivity) factor into pricing decisions?

Potential Solutions and Policy Proposals:

1. **Government Price Negotiation:** Allowing government health programs to negotiate drug prices directly with manufacturers.

2. **International Reference Pricing:** Basing drug prices on what other countries pay.

3. **Value-based Pricing:** Tying drug prices more closely to their demonstrated health benefits.

4. **Increased Competition:** Policies should encourage more competition, including faster approval of generics and

biosimilars.

5. **Transparency Initiatives:** Companies must disclose more information about pricing decisions and R&D costs.

6. **Delinkage Models:** These models separate the cost of R&D from the price of drugs, potentially through prize funds or other alternative funding mechanisms.

7. **Tiered Pricing:** More systematic implementation of tiered pricing strategies to improve access in lower-income countries.

8. **Public-Private Partnerships:** Collaborations to develop drugs for neglected diseases or populations, with agreements on affordable pricing.

Case Studies:

1. **HIV/AIDS Medications:** The global movement to increase access to antiretroviral drugs highlighted both the challenges of high drug prices and the potential for activism and innovative policies to improve access.

2. **Hepatitis C Treatments:** The introduction of highly effective but extremely costly hepatitis C drugs sparked intense debates about drug pricing and rationing of treatment.

3. **COVID-19 Vaccines:** The global pandemic highlighted issues of fair access to vaccines and treatments and the potential for public investment in R&D to influence pricing and access.

As we grapple with the complex issue of drug pricing and access, key questions arise: How can we create a system that continues incentivising innovation while ensuring broad access to essential medicines? What role should governments play in regulating drug prices? And how can we address global disparities in access to medication in an interconnected world?

7. Research Ethics: Balancing Progress and Protection

Pursuing new medical treatments through pharmaceutical research is vital for advancing human health. However, this pursuit must be balanced with robust ethical safeguards to protect research participants and ensure the integrity of the scientific process.

Key Ethical Principles in Research:

1. **Respect for Persons:** Recognizing the autonomy of research participants and protecting those with diminished autonomy.

2. **Beneficence:** Maximizing benefits and minimising harm to research participants and society.

3. **Justice:** Ensuring a fair distribution of the benefits and burdens of research.

4. **Informed Consent:** Ensuring participants understand and voluntarily agree to the risks and benefits of participation.

Ethical Challenges in Pharmaceutical Research:

1. **Placebo Use:** Balancing the scientific need for placebo-controlled trials with the ethical imperative to provide treatment, especially in serious diseases.

2. **Vulnerable Populations:** Adequate protections must be clearly defined for vulnerable groups such as children, pregnant women, the elderly, and people in developing countries.

3. **Post-Trial Access:** Determining the obligations to provide continued access to beneficial treatments after a trial ends,

particularly in resource-poor settings.

4. **Conflict of Interest:** When researchers have commercial interests in the drugs they study, they must manage potential conflicts.

5. **Publication Bias:** Addressing the tendency to publish positive results while suppressing negative ones, which can skew the scientific record.

6. **Data Transparency:** Debates over how much trial data should be publicly available.

7. **Offshoring Clinical Trials:** The ethical implications of conducting trials in developing countries with less stringent regulations.

8. **Animal Testing:** Balancing the need for preclinical animal studies with ethical concerns about animal welfare.

9. **Gene Editing and Advanced Therapies**: Emerging technologies like CRISPR and stem cell therapies are raising new ethical frontiers.

Historical Context and Lessons:

1. **Nuremberg Code:** Set up in response to Nazi atrocities, emphasising voluntary consent and risk minimisation.

2. **Declaration of Helsinki:** Provides ethical principles for medical research involving human subjects.

3. **Tuskegee Syphilis Study:** Unethical study led to increased protections for research participants, predominantly minority populations.

4. **Thalidomide Disaster:** Led to stricter drug testing and approval processes.

Regulatory Framework:

1. **Institutional Review Boards (IRBs)/Ethics Committees:** Oversee research protocols to meet ethical standards.

2. **Good Clinical Practice (GCP):** International ethical and scientific quality clinical trial standards.

3. **Clinical Trials Registration:** Requirements to register trials in public databases to increase transparency.

4. **Informed Consent Processes:** Stringent requirements for obtaining and documenting informed consent from participants.

Emerging Trends and Challenges:

1. **Big Data and AI in Research:** Ethical implications of using large datasets and AI algorithms in drug discovery and clinical research.

2. **Patient-Centered Research:** Increasing involvement of patients in study design and outcome selection.

3. **Adaptive Trial Designs:** These more flexible trial designs can adapt based on interim results, raising new ethical considerations.

4. **Global Health Emergencies:** Ethical challenges in conducting research during outbreaks or pandemics, as seen with COVID-19.

5. **Return of Results:** There are debates over whether and how to return individual research results to participants, especially in genetic studies.

Ethical Considerations:

1. **Balancing Risk and Benefit:** How do we appropriately weigh

potential benefits against risks in clinical research?

2. **Global Justice:** How can we ensure that research benefits and burdens are distributed globally?

3. **Scientific Integrity vs. Commercial Interests:** How do we maintain the integrity of the scientific process in an environment where financial interests are significant?

4. **Cultural Sensitivity:** How can research ethics accommodate cultural perspectives while maintaining core ethical principles?

5. **Future Generations:** What are our ethical obligations to future generations in developing new treatments and preserving research integrity?

As we consider the ethics of pharmaceutical research, key questions emerge: How can we foster a research environment that prioritises patient welfare and scientific integrity while encouraging innovation? How do we balance the need for rigorous scientific evidence with the ethical imperative to provide treatment? And how can we ensure that research benefits are equitably shared across global populations?

8. Intellectual Property: Innovation and Access

Intellectual property rights, particularly patents, are crucial to the pharmaceutical industry's business model. While these rights are intended to incentivise innovation by allowing companies to recoup their R&D investments, they also raise significant issues regarding access to medicines.

Key Aspects of Pharmaceutical Intellectual Property:

1. **Patents:** Patents grant exclusive rights to an invention for a limited period, typically 20 years from the filing date.

2. **Data Exclusivity:** Protects the clinical trial data submitted for drug approval from use by generic competitors for a certain period.

3. **Market Exclusivity** is additional protection granted for certain types of drugs (e.g., orphan drugs) regardless of their patent status.

4. **Trade Secrets:** Used to protect manufacturing processes and other proprietary information.

5. **Trademarks:** Protect brand names and logos associated with drugs.

Challenges and Controversies:

1. **Patent Evergreening:** Strategies companies use to extend patent protection, such as patenting new formulations or uses of existing drugs.

2. **Patent Thickets:** The use of multiple overlapping patents to protect a specific product, potentially hindering competition.

3. **Pay-for-Delay Agreements:** Settlements where brand-name companies pay generic manufacturers to delay market entry.

4. **Compulsory Licensing** is the government-authorized use of patented inventions without the patent holder's consent, which is often controversial in international trade relations.

5. **TRIPS Agreement and Public Health:** There are debates over the flexibility of international IP agreements to address public health crises.

6. **Biopiracy:** Concerns about patenting traditional knowledge or genetic resources without proper consent or benefit-sharing.

7. **Research Tools:** Debates over patenting essential research tools and their impact on further innovation.

Ethical Considerations:

1. **Innovation vs. Access:** How do we balance incentivising innovation with ensuring access to essential medicines?

2. **Global Equity:** How can the IP system address disparities in access to medicines between high and low-income countries?

3. **Open Science vs. Proprietary Research:** What is the appropriate balance between the open sharing of scientific knowledge and the protection of commercial interests?

4. **Fairness in Patent Awards:** How do we ensure that patents reward genuine innovation rather than clever legal strategies?

5. **Public Funding and Private Patents:** What should the IP implications be when public funding contributes to drug development?

Potential Solutions and Policy Proposals:

1. **Patent Pools:** Mechanisms for sharing patents to facilitate the development of new combination therapies or address specific diseases.

2. **Tiered Pricing:** Systematic implementation of differential pricing based on a country's economic status.

3. **Delinkage Models:** These models separate the incentives for R&D from the end product's price, potentially through prize funds or other mechanisms.

4. **Open Source Drug Discovery:** Collaborative approaches to early-stage drug discovery with agreements on downstream IP management.

5. **Socially Responsible Licensing:** Inclusion of access provisions in university technology transfer agreements.

6. **Reform of Patent Laws:** Proposals to modify patent laws to discourage evergreening and promote genuine innovation.

7. **Alternative R&D Funding Models:** Increased public funding or public-private partnerships for drug development with agreements on IP management and pricing.

Case Studies:

1. **HIV/AIDS Medications:** Compulsory licensing and activist pressure led to increased access to antiretroviral drugs in low and middle-income countries.

2. **Hepatitis C Treatments:** High prices protected by patents led to rationing of highly effective new treatments, sparking debates about IP and access.

3. **CRISPR Gene Editing:** Patent disputes over this breakthrough technology highlight the complexities of IP in innovative biomedical research.

As we navigate the complex landscape of pharmaceutical intellectual property, key questions emerge: How can we design IP systems that foster genuine innovation while ensuring global access to essential medicines? What alternative models might better balance the interests of innovators, patients, and society? And how can we adapt IP frameworks to address emerging challenges like personalised medicine and advanced therapies?

9. Globalization and Global Health: Challenges and Opportunities

The pharmaceutical industry operates globally, which has significant implications for business practices and global health outcomes. This international nature presents opportunities for addressing worldwide health challenges and complex ethical dilemmas.

Key Aspects of Pharmaceutical Globalization:

1. **Global Supply Chains:** Raw materials, manufacturing, and distribution often span multiple countries.

2. **International Clinical Trials:** Research is increasingly conducted across borders, often in developing countries.

3. **Emerging Markets:** Growing focus on expanding into developing countries with large populations.

4. **Regulatory Harmonization:** Efforts to align drug approval processes across countries.

5. **Global Health Initiatives:** Involvement in international efforts to address significant health challenges.

6. **Cross-border Mergers and Acquisitions:** Consolidation of the industry globally.

Challenges and Controversies:

1. **Access Disparities:** Significant differences in access to medicines between high and low-income countries.

2. **Neglected Diseases:** Lack of R&D for diseases primarily affecting low-income populations.

3. **Counterfeit Medicines:** Global trade in fake or substandard drugs, particularly affecting developing countries.

4. **Regulatory Arbitrage:** Companies potentially exploiting differences in national regulations.

5. **Clinical Trial Ethics:** Concerns about the ethics of

conducting trials in countries with weaker regulatory frameworks.

6. **Brain Drain:** Healthcare professionals and researchers move from developing to developed countries.

7. **Trade Agreements and Health:** Impact of international trade agreements on access to medicines and health policies.

Ethical Considerations:

1. **Global Justice:** How can the benefits and burdens of pharmaceutical research and development be fairly distributed globally?

2. **Cultural Sensitivity:** How can global pharmaceutical practices respect local cultural norms and health traditions?

3. **Post-trial Obligations:** What responsibilities do companies have to trial participants and communities after research concludes?

4. **Pricing and Access:** How can pricing strategies balance profitability with global access to essential medicines?

5. **Local Capacity Building:** What role should multinational pharmaceutical companies play in building healthcare and research capacity in developing countries?

Potential Solutions and Initiatives:

1. **Tiered Pricing:** Systematic implementation of differential pricing based on a country's economic status.

2. **Product Development Partnerships:** Collaborations between industry, academia, and non-profits to address neglected diseases.

3. **Advance Market Commitments:** Guarantees to purchase

vaccines or drugs for developing countries to incentivise their development.

4. **Technology Transfer:** Sharing manufacturing know-how to build local production capacity in developing countries.

5. **Global Health Security:** Initiatives to prepare for and respond to global health emergencies, including stockpiling essential medicines.

6. **Strengthening Regulatory Systems:** Efforts to build robust drug regulatory capacities in developing countries.

7. **Open-Source Drug Discovery:** International collaborative approaches to early-stage drug discovery for neglected diseases.

Case Studies:

1. **Global HIV/AIDS Response:** Highlighted the challenges of high drug prices and the potential for global cooperation to improve access.

2. **Ebola Vaccine Development:** Highlighted the complexities of developing treatments for emerging infectious diseases affecting primarily low-income countries.

3. **COVID-19 Pandemic:** Demonstrated the potential for rapid global scientific collaboration and the challenges of ensuring equitable access to vaccines and treatments.

As we consider the global dimensions of the pharmaceutical industry, key questions emerge: How can we create a more equitable global system for drug development and access? What responsibilities do pharmaceutical companies have to address global health challenges beyond their primary markets? How can international pharmaceutical research and development cooperation be fostered while respecting national sovereignty and local needs?

10. **The Future of Pharmaceuticals: Trends and Ethical Horizons**

Looking to the future, several emerging trends promise to reshape the pharmaceutical landscape, each bringing ethical challenges and opportunities.

Emerging Trends:

1. **Personalized Medicine:**

   - Tailoring treatments to individual genetic profiles.

   - Ethical issues: privacy concerns, potential for genetic discrimination, fair access.

2. **Gene Therapy and Editing:**

   - Potential to cure genetic diseases at their source.

   - Ethical issues: safety concerns, germline modifications, enhancement vs. therapy debates.

3. **Artificial Intelligence in Drug Discovery:**

   - Using AI to accelerate drug discovery and development processes.

   - Ethical issues: data privacy, potential biases in AI algorithms, accountability for AI-driven decisions.

4. **Digital Therapeutics:**

   - Software-based interventions to prevent, manage, or treat medical disorders.

   - Ethical issues: data security, regulatory challenges, impact on traditional healthcare roles.

5. **3D Printing of Drugs:**

- Potential for on-demand, personalised drug production.

- Ethical issues: quality control, regulatory oversight, potential for misuse.

6. **Nanotechnology:**

- Targeted drug delivery at the molecular level.

- Ethical issues: long-term safety concerns and environmental impact.

7. **Microbiome-based Therapies:**

- Leveraging gut bacteria for therapeutic effects.

- Ethical issues: safety, long-term impacts on human biology.

8. **Psychedelic Medicine:**

- Renewed interest in psychedelic substances for mental health treatment.

- Ethical issues: potential for abuse, appropriate use and regulation.

9. **Global Health Security:**

- Increased focus on preparing for future pandemics.

- Ethical issues: equitable distribution of resources, balancing national interests with global needs.

10. **Sustainable Pharmaceuticals:**

- Growing emphasis on environmental sustainability in drug production and disposal.

- Ethical issues: balancing environmental concerns with medical needs and responsibility for environmental impacts.

Ethical Challenges and Considerations:

1. **Redefining "Health" and "Disease":** As our ability to intervene at the genetic and molecular level grows, how do we define what constitutes a disease requiring treatment versus normal human variation?

2. **Enhancement vs. Therapy:** Where do we draw the line between treating illness and enhancing human capabilities?

3. **Data Privacy and Ownership:** As personalised medicine and AI-driven healthcare become more prevalent, how do we protect individual privacy while harnessing the power of big data for medical advances?

4. **Equitable Access:** How can we ensure that cutting-edge treatments are not limited to only the wealthiest individuals or nations?

5. **Responsible Innovation:** How do we balance the drive for rapid scientific progress with the need for careful safety evaluation and ethical consideration?

6. **Global Cooperation:** How can we foster international collaboration in pharmaceutical research and development while respecting national interests in an increasingly interconnected world?

7. **Environmental Stewardship:** How can the pharmaceutical industry minimise its environmental impact without compromising medical innovation and production?

8. **Artificial Intelligence Ethics:** As AI plays an increasing role in drug discovery and healthcare decisions, how do we ensure transparency, accountability, and the elimination of bias?

9. **Human Dignity and Autonomy:** How do we preserve human dignity and autonomy in an era of increasingly sophisticated medical interventions?

10. **Intergenerational Justice:** How do we balance the needs and rights of current patients with our responsibilities to future generations, particularly in areas like genetic modification?

Potential Ethical Frameworks and Approaches:

1. **Anticipatory Ethics** involves proactively considering the ethical implications of emerging technologies before they are fully developed and deployed.

2. **Global Ethics:** Developing ethical frameworks to address the global nature of pharmaceutical research and distribution.

3. **Participatory Technology Assessment:** This involves diverse stakeholders, including patients and the general public, in discussions about the direction of pharmaceutical research and development.

4. **Rights-Based Approaches:** Grounding pharmaceutical ethics in fundamental human rights, including the right to health and to benefit from scientific progress.

5. **Virtue Ethics in Pharma:** Encouraging the cultivation of virtues like compassion, integrity, and justice within the pharmaceutical industry and among healthcare providers.

6. **Ethical AI Design:** Developing principles and practices for AI's ethical design and use in pharmaceutical research and healthcare.

7. **Environmental Ethics:** Integrating considerations of environmental sustainability into pharmaceutical ethics.

Policy and Governance Considerations:

1. **Adaptive Regulation:** Developing regulatory frameworks to keep pace with rapid technological change while ensuring safety and ethical standards.

2. **Global Governance Structures:** Creating or strengthening international bodies to address global pharmaceutical challenges and ethics.

3. **Public-Private Partnerships:** Fostering collaborations between industry, government, and non-profit sectors to address significant health challenges ethically and effectively.

4. **Ethics Education:** Enhancing ethics training for scientists, healthcare providers, and pharmaceutical industry professionals.

5. **Transparency Initiatives:** Promoting greater transparency in pharmaceutical research, development, and marketing.

6. **Ethical Investment**: Encouraging investment strategies prioritising ethical and sustainable pharmaceutical practices.

Case Studies for the Future:

1. **CRISPR Babies:** The 2018 case of genetically edited babies in China gives a stark example of the ethical challenges we may face as gene editing technologies advance.

2. **AI Drug Discovery:** The use of AI to identify potential COVID-19 treatments showcases both the promise and the ethical considerations of AI in pharmaceuticals.

3. **Psychedelic Therapy:** The resurgence of interest in psychedelic substances for mental health treatment raises questions about drug policy, mental health treatment paradigms, and the boundaries of medical intervention.

Conclusion:

We are called upon to navigate complex ethical terrain as we stand on the brink of transformative advances in pharmaceutical science and technology. The potential to alleviate suffering and extend human life has never been more significant, but neither have the risks of unintended consequences or misuse of powerful modern technologies.

Fostering ongoing dialogue between scientists, ethicists, policymakers, and the public will be crucial. We must strive to create systems and practices that harness the immense potential of pharmaceutical innovation while steadfastly upholding human dignity, promoting global equity, and safeguarding the interests of current and future generations.

The future of pharmaceuticals offers a profound opportunity to redefine our approach to health, disease, and human flourishing. By thoughtfully engaging with the ethical dimensions of these advances, we can work towards a future where the power of modern medicine is wielded responsibly and ethically for the benefit of all humanity.

11. Conclusion: Balancing Profit, Innovation, and Public Health

As we conclude our exploration of Big Pharma, we grapple with a complex landscape of competing interests, ethical dilemmas, and profound human impact. The pharmaceutical industry stands at a critical juncture, facing unprecedented opportunities to improve human health and significant challenges to its current practices and business models.

Recap of Key Themes:

1. The tension between profit-driven business models and public health needs.

2. Drug development's high costs and risks and their impact on pricing and access.

3. The ethical challenges in research, marketing, and global operations.

4. Intellectual property rights' crucial role in incentivising innovation and potentially limiting access.

5. The global nature of the industry and its implications for addressing worldwide health challenges.

6. The transformative potential of emerging technologies and the ethical questions they raise.

Moving forward, several key principles might guide our approach to pharmaceutical ethics and policy:

1. **Prioritizing Patient Welfare:** Ensure that pharmaceuticals' fundamental purpose—to heal and alleviate suffering—remains paramount in all industry practices.

2. **Fostering Genuine Innovation:** Encouraging research that addresses unmet medical needs rather than merely tweaking existing products for commercial gain.

3. **Ensuring Global Access:** Developing systems and practices that make essential medicines available to all who need them, regardless of economic status.

4. **Promoting Transparency:** Encouraging openness in pharmaceutical research, development, and marketing to build trust and enable informed decision-making.

5. **Balancing Incentives:** Creating frameworks that reward innovation while preventing excessive profiteering at the expense of public health.

6. **Embracing Ethical Technology:** Harnessing the power of modern technologies like AI and gene editing in ways that respect human dignity and promote equity.

7. **Environmental Responsibility:** Integrating environmental sustainability considerations into all pharmaceutical production and distribution aspects.

8. **Global Cooperation:** Fostering international collaboration to address significant health challenges while respecting national sovereignty and local needs.

9. **Ethical Governance:** Developing adaptive regulatory frameworks that can keep pace with technological change while upholding ethical standards.

10. **Stakeholder Engagement:** The future of pharmaceuticals will be shaped by diverse voices, including patients, healthcare providers, and the public.

The path forward will require difficult trade-offs and careful balancing acts. We must find ways to maintain the innovative potential of the pharmaceutical industry while curbing its excesses and ensuring its tremendous power is wielded for the greater good.

This may involve exploring new business models, alternative funding mechanisms for research, more collaborative approaches to drug development, and innovative pricing strategies. It will undoubtedly require ongoing dialogue between industry, government, academia, healthcare providers, and the public.

As we navigate these challenges, we might draw wisdom from various ethical traditions, including ancient philosophical and spiritual teachings. The emphasis on compassion, justice, and the interconnectedness of all beings in many of these traditions could offer valuable guidance as we align the pharmaceutical industry more closely with the highest aspirations of medicine and public health.

Ultimately, Big Pharma's story is a human story. It's about our quest to understand and heal the human body, our struggle with the ethical implications of our growing powers, and our ongoing effort to balance individual and collective needs. It reflects both the noblest aspects of human ingenuity and compassion and the challenges of greed and short-sightedness. As we look to the future, we are called upon to exercise our uniquely human abilities for ethical reasoning, foresight, and collective action. Our choices about structuring and regulating the pharmaceutical industry will have profound implications for human health, global equity, and our relationship with emerging technologies.

In conclusion, while the challenges facing Big Pharma are significant, they also present an opportunity to reimagine and reshape one of the most important industries of our time. By approaching these issues with wisdom, ethical commitment, and a spirit of global cooperation, we can work towards a future where the immense power of modern pharmaceuticals is harnessed more effectively and ethically for the benefit of all humanity. The healing or hubris of Big Pharma is not predetermined—it is in our hands to shape it.

CHAPTER 7: ADVERTISING: THE ART OF EGO MANIPULATION

1. Introduction: The Pervasive Power of Advertising

In the modern world, advertising is an omnipresent force that subtly and overtly shapes our beliefs, desires, and behaviours. From billboards and television commercials to sponsored content on social media, advertising has become an inescapable part of our daily lives. This chapter explores the complex relationship between advertising and the human ego, examining how the industry taps into our deepest insecurities, aspirations, and sense of self to influence our consumer behaviour.

As we delve into this topic, we will trace the evolution of advertising from simple product announcements to sophisticated, multi-platform campaigns that blur the lines between entertainment, information, and persuasion. We will examine the psychological tactics employed by advertisers, the ethical implications of these practices, and the broader societal impacts of a culture saturated in commercial messages.

Throughout our exploration, we will consider how advertising intersects with identity, self-esteem, and social status issues. We will examine how different demographic groups are targeted and affected by advertising and how the industry both reflects and shapes cultural values.

We will also examine the changing landscape of advertising in the digital age, including the rise of personalised ads, influencer marketing, and the use of big data and artificial intelligence in ad targeting. These technological developments raise new ethical questions and challenges for both advertisers and consumers.

As we navigate this complex topic, we will draw on insights from psychology, sociology, economics, and media studies. We will also consider perspectives from various ethical frameworks, including those found in ancient wisdom traditions and religious texts, which may offer valuable counterpoints to the often short-term, materialistic focus of much advertising.

By understanding the mechanisms and impacts of advertising, we can develop a more critical and conscious relationship with the commercial messages that surround us. This awareness is crucial not only for our individual well-being but also for addressing broader societal issues related to consumerism, environmental sustainability, and social equity.

2. The Evolution of Advertising: From Information to Persuasion

To understand the current state of advertising and its impact on the ego, it's essential to trace its historical development. The practice of advertising has transformed dramatically over time, reflecting and driving changes in technology, media, and social attitudes.

Early Beginnings:

- **Ancient times:** Simple announcements or signs for products or services.

- **Middle Ages:** Town criers and signboards for local businesses.

- **15th-17th centuries:** Rise of print advertising with the invention of the printing press.

Industrial Revolution and Mass Production:

- Late 18th-19th centuries: Increased production capabilities led to a need for broader market reach.

- Rise of newspapers and magazines as advertising platforms.

- Development of trademarks and brand identities.

The Golden Age of Advertising:

- Early-mid 20th century: Radio and then television revolutionized advertising reach and impact.

- 1920s-1960s: Emergence of modern advertising agencies and techniques.

- Shift from product-focused to lifestyle-focused advertising.

The Creative Revolution:

- 1960s-1970s: Emphasis on creativity and unique selling propositions.

- Iconic campaigns that played with audience expectations and emotions.

The Digital Revolution:

- 1990s-present: Internet advertising, from banner ads to sophisticated targeted marketing.

- Rise of social media platforms as major advertising channels.

- Big data and AI-driven personalization of ads.

Key Transformations:

1. **From Information to Persuasion:** Early ads were primarily informational; modern ads often focus on emotional appeals and lifestyle associations.

2. **Expansion of Media Channels:** From print to radio, TV, internet, and mobile devices, each new medium has changed how ads are created and consumed.

3. **Targeting and Personalization:** From mass market approaches to highly targeted, personalized advertising.

4. **Integration with Content:** From clear separation of ads and content to native advertising and branded content.

5. **Interactivity:** From passive consumption to interactive and immersive advertising experiences.

6. **Globalization:** From local to national to global advertising campaigns.

7. **Measurement and Analytics:** From broad estimates of reach to precise tracking of engagement and conversion.

This historical trajectory raises important questions: How has the evolution of advertising shaped our relationship with consumption and our sense of self? Has the increasing sophistication of advertising techniques enhanced or eroded consumer autonomy? And how might understanding this history inform our approach to the ethical challenges posed by modern advertising?

3. The Psychology of Advertising: Tapping into the Ego

At the heart of effective advertising lies a deep understanding of human psychology, particularly the workings of the ego. Advertisers employ a range of psychological tactics to influence consumer behavior, often by appealing to or manipulating aspects of our self-concept and emotional needs.

Key Psychological Concepts in Advertising:

1. Self-Image and Ideal Self:

- Ads often appeal to our desire to bridge the gap between our actual self and ideal self.

- Products are presented as means to become the person we aspire to be.

2. Social Comparison:

- Advertising frequently triggers comparison with others, playing on our desire for status and belonging.

- FOMO (Fear of Missing Out) is a common tactic, especially in social media advertising.

3. Emotional Appeals:

- Ads aim to evoke emotions like happiness, nostalgia, fear, or excitement, associating these feelings with products.

- Emotional connections can be more persuasive than rational arguments.

4. Cognitive Dissonance:

- Ads can create or resolve cognitive dissonance, motivating purchases to align beliefs and actions.

5. Maslow's Hierarchy of Needs:

- Advertisements often target different levels of Maslow's hierarchy, from basic needs to self-actualization.

6. **Conditioning and Association:**

- Classical conditioning techniques are used to associate positive feelings or desirable traits with products.

7. **Scarcity and Exclusivity:**

- Creating a sense of scarcity or exclusivity appeals to our ego's desire for uniqueness and status.

8. **Social Proof:**

- Testimonials, influencer endorsements, and "bestseller" claims leverage our tendency to follow others' leads.

9. **Narrative Transportation:**

- Engaging storytelling in ads can transport viewers mentally, making them more receptive to persuasion.

10. **Ego Depletion:**

- Ads may target moments when our self-control is weakened, such as late at night or when stressed.

<u>Targeting Different Aspects of the Ego:</u>

1. **Identity**: Ads that appeal to our sense of who we are or want to be (e.g., eco-friendly products for those who identify as environmentally conscious).

2. **Self-esteem:** Products presented as means to boost confidence or social standing.

3. **Belongingness:** Advertising that plays on our need to fit in with certain groups or subcultures.

4. **Achievement:** Ads that associate products with success and accomplishment.

5. **Control:** Marketing that suggests products can help us gain control over our lives or environment.

6. **Security:** Advertisements that appeal to our need for safety and stability.

Ethical Considerations:

1. **Manipulation vs. Persuasion:** Where is the line between legitimate persuasion and unethical manipulation of psychological vulnerabilities?

2. **Informed Consent:** To what extent are consumers aware of and able to resist psychological tactics used in advertising?

3. **Vulnerable Populations:** How do we protect groups that may be particularly susceptible to certain advertising techniques, such as children or those with mental health issues?

4. **Truth in Advertising:** How can psychological appeals be balanced with honest representation of products?

5. **Long-Term Well-being:** What are the cumulative psychological effects of constant exposure to ego-targeted advertising?

As we consider the psychology of advertising, key questions emerge: How can consumers become more aware of and resilient to psychological manipulation in advertising? What ethical guidelines should govern the use of psychological tactics in marketing? And how might we create a marketing landscape that respects psychological well-being while still allowing for effective commercial communication?

4. Digital Advertising: The New Frontier of Ego Manipulation

The digital revolution has transformed advertising, opening up new avenues for targeting consumers and manipulating the ego. This section explores the unique features of digital advertising and their implications for individual psychology and society at large.

Key Features of Digital Advertising:

1. Personalization and Targeting:

   - Use of personal data to tailor ads to individual preferences and behaviors.

   - Retargeting based on previous online activity.

2. Interactive and Immersive Experiences:

   - Augmented reality (AR) and virtual reality (VR) ads allowing for deeper engagement.

   - Interactive ads that respond to user input.

3. Native Advertising and Sponsored Content:

   - Ads that blend seamlessly with non-advertising content.

   - Influencer marketing on social media platforms.

4. Real-Time Bidding and Programmatic Advertising:

   - Automated buying and selling of ad space in real-time.

   - Allows for highly specific targeting based on user data.

5. Multi-Platform Campaigns:

   - Coordinated advertising across devices and platforms.

- Cross-device tracking to create comprehensive user profiles.

6. Social Media Advertising:

   - Leveraging social networks for viral marketing.

   - Ads integrated into social feeds and stories.

7. Artificial Intelligence and Machine Learning:

   - AI-driven ad creation and optimization.

   - Predictive analytics to anticipate consumer behavior.

Psychological Impacts of Digital Advertising:

1. Filter Bubbles and Echo Chambers:

   - Personalized ads can reinforce existing beliefs and preferences, potentially narrowing perspectives.

2. Constant Exposure:

   - The ubiquity of digital ads can lead to ad fatigue or, conversely, unconscious influence.

3. Blurring of Reality and Advertising:

   - Native ads and influencer marketing can make it difficult to distinguish genuine content from advertising.

4. Instant Gratification:

   - One-click purchasing and personalized offers can encourage impulsive buying.

5. FOMO and Social Comparison:

   - Social media advertising often leverages fear of missing out and social comparison.

6. Data Privacy Concerns:

- Awareness of data collection for ad targeting can lead to feelings of vulnerability or loss of privacy.

7. Addiction and Compulsive Behavior:

- Some digital advertising techniques, particularly in mobile apps and games, can encourage addictive patterns.

Ethical Considerations:

1. Data Privacy: How can we balance the benefits of personalization with the right to privacy?

2. Informed Consent: Are users truly aware of how their data is being used for advertising purposes?

3. Addiction: What responsibility do advertisers have in designing non-addictive ad experiences?

4. Child Protection: How can we shield children from manipulative digital advertising practices?

5. Truth in Advertising: How can we maintain transparency in native advertising and influencer marketing?

6. Digital Divide: How does the shift to digital advertising affect those with limited internet access or digital literacy?

7. Algorithmic Bias: How can we ensure that AI-driven advertising doesn't perpetuate or exacerbate social biases?

Potential Future and Concerning Trends:

1. Voice-Activated Advertising: How will advertising adapt as smart speakers and voice assistants become more prevalent?

2. Internet of Things (IoT) Advertising: How will ads be integrated into smart home devices and other IoT technologies?

3. Neuromarketing: The potential use of brain scanning and other neurological data in advertising raises new ethical questions.

4. Blockchain in Advertising: Could blockchain technology provide more transparency and control over personal data in advertising?

As we navigate the rapidly evolving landscape of digital advertising, key questions emerge: How can we harness the benefits of personalisation and technological innovation while protecting individual autonomy and well-being? What new literacy skills do consumers need to engage with digital advertising critically? And how might regulatory frameworks need to evolve to address the unique challenges posed by digital advertising technologies?

5. Advertising and Identity: Shaping the Self through Consumption

Advertising plays a significant role in shaping how we view ourselves and construct our identities. By associating products and brands with particular lifestyles, values, and personality traits, advertising suggests that we can build and express our identities through consumption.

Key Aspects of Advertising and Identity:

1. Brand Identity and Personal Identity:

- Brands often position themselves as embodiments of certain values or lifestyles.

- Consumers may adopt these brand identities as part of

their personal identity.

2. Aspirational Marketing:

   - Ads that show idealized versions of life, suggesting that products can help achieve these ideals.

   - Appeals to the "ideal self" rather than the "actual self."

3. Segmentation and Targeting:

   - Ads tailored to specific demographic groups, reinforcing or challenging identity categories.

   - Micro-targeting based on detailed personal data, potentially reinforcing niche identities.

4. Cultural Identity:

   - Advertising both reflects and shapes cultural norms and values.

   - Global brands may promote a homogenized global identity, while others emphasize local or national identities.

5. Gender and Sexuality:

   - Ads often reinforce or challenge gender norms and sexual identities.

   - Increasing representation of diverse gender identities and sexual orientations in advertising.

6. Age and Generational Identity:

   - Different advertising approaches for different age groups, often playing on generational characteristics.

7. Social Status and Class Identity:

- Luxury advertising appeals to desires for status and class mobility.

- Some brands build identity around rejecting traditional status symbols.

8. Professional Identity:

- Ads that tie products to career success or professional image.

9. Body Image:

- Beauty and fitness product advertising shapes ideals of physical appearance.

10. Digital Identity:

- Social media advertising intertwines with how we present ourselves online.

Psychological Mechanisms:

1. Social Comparison Theory:

- Ads often trigger comparison with idealized others, influencing self-evaluation.

2. Self-Discrepancy Theory:

- Advertising can highlight gaps between actual, ideal, and ought selves, motivating consumption to reduce these discrepancies.

3. Identity Salience:

- Ads can make certain aspects of identity more prominent, influencing behaviour.

4. Symbolic Interactionism:

- Products are presented as symbols that communicate identity to others.

Ethical Considerations:

1. Authenticity: How does advertising-influenced identity construction affect authentic self-expression?

2. Diversity and Representation: What responsibilities do advertisers have in representing diverse identities?

3. Stereotyping: How can advertising avoid reinforcing harmful stereotypes while still effectively targeting specific groups?

4. Materialism: What are the implications of tying identity so closely to material consumption?

5. Child and Adolescent Identity Formation: How does advertising impact young people's identity development?

6. Cultural Appropriation: How can global advertising respect cultural identities without exploiting or misrepresenting them?

7. Digital Footprints: What are the long-term implications of constructing identity through trackable online consumer behaviour?

Case Studies:

1. Nike's "Just Do It" campaign: Tying athletic products to a broader identity of determination and achievement.

2. Dove's "Real Beauty" campaign: Challenging traditional beauty standards while promoting beauty products.

3. Apple's "Think Different" campaign: Associating technology products with creativity and non-conformity.

As we consider the relationship between advertising and identity, key questions emerge: How can individuals maintain a sense of authentic self in a world saturated with identity-shaping advertisements? What role should advertisers play in promoting positive, diverse representations of identity? And how might we create a culture that values identity formation based on internal values and experiences rather than consumer choices?

6. The Ethics of Persuasion: Manipulation or Communication?

The practice of advertising raises fundamental ethical questions about the nature of persuasion and the boundaries between legitimate communication and manipulation. This section explores the ethical dimensions of advertising tactics and their impact on individual autonomy and societal well-being.

Key Ethical Issues in Advertising:

1. Truth and Deception:

  - False or misleading claims in advertising.

  - Omission of essential information.

  - Use of fine print or confusing language.

2. Manipulation of Emotions:

  - Exploiting fears, insecurities, or desires.

  - Creating artificial needs or problems.

3. Targeting Vulnerable Groups:

  - Advertising to children.

- Marketing potentially harmful products (e.g., alcohol, gambling) to at-risk populations.

4. Privacy and Data Use:

   - Collection and use of personal data for targeted advertising.

   - Transparency about data collection practices.

5. Social Responsibility:

   - Promoting harmful stereotypes or unrealistic body images.

   - Environmental impact of promoting excessive consumption.

6. Subliminal Advertising:

   - Use of messages below the threshold of conscious awareness.

7. Native Advertising and Sponsored Content:

   - Blurring lines between editorial content and advertising.

8. Political Advertising:

   - Truthfulness and transparency in political ads.

   - Microtargeting of political messages.

Ethical Frameworks for Evaluating Advertising:

1. Kantian Ethics:

   - Respecting the autonomy of individuals and not treating them merely as means.

   - Question: Does the ad respect the consumer's ability to make rational decisions?

2. Utilitarianism:

- Considering the overall societal impact of advertising practices.

- Question: Does the ad contribute to greater overall well-being or harm?

3. Virtue Ethics:

- Focusing on the character and intentions of advertisers.

- Question: Does the ad reflect virtues such as honesty, integrity, and compassion?

4. Social Contract Theory:

- Considering what advertising practices a society would collectively agree to.

- Question: Would these advertising tactics be acceptable in a fair and just society?

5. Care Ethics:

- Emphasizing relationships and responsibilities.

- Question: Does the ad respect and nurture the relationship between brand and consumer?

6. Rights-based Ethics:

- Focusing on individual rights such as privacy and informed consent.

- Question: Does the ad respect the fundamental rights of consumers?

Ethical Guidelines and Self-Regulation:

1. Truth in Advertising Laws: Legal requirements for honesty in advertising claims.

2. Industry Self-Regulation: Voluntary codes of conduct adopted by advertising associations.

3. Corporate Ethics Policies: Individual company guidelines for ethical advertising practices.

4. Media Guidelines: Standards set by media outlets for acceptable advertising content.

Challenges in Ethical Advertising:

1. Balancing Creativity and Truth: How to create engaging ads without crossing ethical lines.

2. Cultural Differences: Navigating different ethical norms across global markets.

3. Technological Advancements: Keeping ethical standards up to date with new advertising technologies.

4. Competitive Pressure: Supporting ethical standards in a highly competitive market.

5. Measuring Impact: Difficulty in assessing the long-term societal effects of advertising practices.

Case Studies:

1. Tobacco Advertising: The ethical implications of marketing harmful products.

2. Body Image in Fashion Advertising: The impact of unrealistic beauty standards.

3. Green Washing: Misleading environmental claims in advertising.

4. Influencer Marketing: Disclosure and authenticity in social media promotions.

Potential Solutions and Best Practices:

1. Enhanced Transparency: Clear disclosure of advertising intent and sponsorship.

2. Ethical Review Boards: Independent bodies to evaluate advertising campaigns.

3. Consumer Education: Initiatives to improve media literacy and critical thinking skills.

4. Ethical AI in Advertising: Developing guidelines for the use of AI in ad targeting and creation.

5. Stakeholder Engagement: Involving consumers, ethicists, and other stakeholders in developing advertising standards.

As we navigate the complex ethical landscape of advertising, key questions emerge: How can we create a system that allows for effective commercial communication while respecting consumer autonomy and well-being? What role should government regulation play versus industry self-regulation? And how can we foster a culture of ethical advertising that goes beyond mere compliance with rules to truly prioritize social responsibility?

7. Advertising and Society: Shaping Cultural Values and Norms

Advertising doesn't just reflect society; it plays a significant role in shaping cultural values, norms, and aspirations. This section explores the broader societal impacts of advertising, both positive and negative.

Advertising's Influence on Society:

1. Consumerism and Materialism:

   - Promotion of consumption as a path to happiness and fulfillment.

   - Impact on definitions of success and status.

2. Gender Roles and Stereotypes:

   - Reinforcement or challenge of traditional gender norms.

   - Representation of diverse gender identities and roles.

3. Body Image and Beauty Standards:

   - Influence on ideals of physical attractiveness.

   - Impact on self-esteem and body satisfaction, particularly among young people.

4. Cultural Diversity and Representation:

   - Portrayal of different ethnic and cultural groups.

   - Potential for both promoting diversity and reinforcing stereotypes.

5. Environmental Attitudes:

   - Promotion of eco-friendly products and sustainable practices.

   - Contribution to overconsumption and waste.

6. Social Issues and Activism:

   - Use of advertising to raise awareness about social causes.

- "Woke washing" and the commodification of social movements.

7. Family Structures and Relationships:

   - Depiction of family life and interpersonal relationships.

   - Influence on expectations about love, marriage, and family.

8. Work and Success:

   - Shaping perceptions of career success and work-life balance.

   - Promotion of entrepreneurship and "hustle culture."

9. Technology and Innovation:

   - Driving adoption of new technologies.

   - Shaping expectations about the role of technology in daily life.

10. Health and Wellness:

   - Promotion of health products and lifestyle choices.

   - Potential for both health education and misinformation.

Positive Societal Impacts:

1. Public Health Campaigns: Using advertising techniques for social good (e.g., anti-smoking campaigns).

2. Economic Growth: Stimulating economic activity and job creation.

3. Product Information: Informing consumers about new products and services.

4. Cultural Exchange: Exposing people to different cultures and lifestyles.

5. Social Change: Challenging outdated norms and promoting progressive values.

Negative Societal Impacts:

1. Overconsumption: Encouraging unsustainable levels of consumption.

2. Social Comparison and Dissatisfaction: Fostering feelings of inadequacy and constant comparison.

3. Homogenization of Culture: Promoting a global consumer culture at the expense of local traditions.

4. Information Overload: Contributing to mental fatigue and decision paralysis.

5. Political Polarization: Microtargeting of political ads potentially exacerbating social divisions.

Ethical Considerations:

1. Social Responsibility: What obligations do advertisers have to promote positive societal values?

2. Cultural Sensitivity: How can global advertising respect and preserve local cultures?

3. Truth and Transparency: How can advertising maintain honesty while presenting idealized images?

4. Power Dynamics: How does advertising reinforce or challenge existing power structures in society?

5. Long-term Societal Health: How do we balance short-term commercial interests with long-term societal well-being?

Case Studies:

1. Gillette's "The Best Men Can Be" Campaign: Addressing toxic masculinity and sparking societal debate.

2. Coca-Cola's "Share a Coke" Campaign: Personalizing mass consumption and fostering social connections.

3. Airbnb's "We Accept" Campaign: Promoting diversity and inclusion in response to social issues.

Future Trends and Challenges:

1. Increasing Role of AI: Potential for hyper-personalized advertising to shape individual worldviews.

2. Virtual and Augmented Reality: New immersive advertising experiences blurring lines between reality and marketing.

3. Advertising in Public Spaces: Balancing commercial interests with preservation of public spaces.

4. Global vs. Local: Navigating the tension between global brand consistency and local cultural relevance.

As we consider the societal impact of advertising, key questions emerge: How can we harness the power of advertising to promote positive social values while mitigating its potential negative effects? What responsibility do advertisers have in shaping cultural norms and values? And how can society maintain a critical distance from advertising messages while still benefiting from their informative aspects?

8. Children and Advertising: Protecting Vulnerable Minds

Advertising targeted at children raises particular ethical concerns due to children's developmental vulnerabilities and limited ability to critically evaluate marketing messages. This section explores the unique challenges and considerations surrounding advertising to young audiences.

Key Issues in Children's Advertising:

1. Cognitive Development:

   - Children's limited ability to distinguish advertising from other content.

   - Developmental stages in understanding persuasive intent.

2. Pester Power:

   - Ads encouraging children to nag parents for products.

   - Impact on family dynamics and parental authority.

3. Childhood Obesity:

   - Role of food advertising in children's dietary choices.

   - Marketing of unhealthy foods and beverages to children.

4. Materialism and Values:

   - Influence on children's developing value systems.

   - Promotion of consumerism from an early age.

5. Digital Advertising:

   - Challenges of regulating online ads targeted at children.

   - In-app purchases and advergames.

6. Data Collection:

   - Privacy concerns related to tracking children's online behavior for advertising purposes.

7. Body Image and Self-Esteem:

- Impact of idealized images in ads on children's self-perception.

- Gender stereotyping in children's advertising.

8. Educational Content:

- Blurring lines between educational material and advertising.

- Sponsored content in schools.

Regulatory Approaches:

1. Government Regulations:

- Restrictions on advertising during children's programming.

- Rules about product placement in children's content.

2. Industry Self-Regulation:

- Voluntary guidelines adopted by advertisers and media companies.

- Pledges to limit marketing of unhealthy foods to children.

3. International Variations:

- Differences in regulations across countries (e.g., stricter rules in Scandinavian countries).

4. Digital-Specific Regulations:

- COPPA (Children's Online Privacy Protection Act) in the U.S.

- EU's GDPR provisions for children's data.

Ethical Considerations:

1. Informed Consent: Children's inability to provide meaningful consent to marketing tactics.

2. Exploitation: The ethics of targeting a vulnerable and impressionable audience.

3. Long-term Impact: Potential effects of early advertising exposure on lifelong consumer behavior.

4. Parental Rights: Balancing parental authority with commercial free speech.

5. Educational Value: Potential positive uses of advertising for children's learning and development.

Strategies for Responsible Advertising to Children:

1. Age-Appropriate Content: Tailoring ads to children's developmental stages.

2. Clear Separation: Maintaining distinct boundaries between advertising and other content.

3. Positive Messaging: Promoting pro-social values and healthy behaviors.

4. Parental Involvement: Providing tools and information for parents to mediate children's advertising exposure.

5. Media Literacy Education: Teaching children to critically evaluate media messages.

Case Studies:

1. Happy Meal Toys: Debates over using toys to market fast food to children.

2. Influencer Marketing to Kids: Ethical implications of child influencers promoting products.

3. Educational Apps: Balancing learning content with in-app advertising and purchases.

Future Challenges:

1. Virtual Reality and Children: Ethical considerations for immersive advertising experiences.

2. AI and Personalization: Implications of AI-driven personalized advertising for child audiences.

3. Global Reach: Addressing disparities in child advertising protections across different countries.

As we consider the intersection of children and advertising, key questions emerge: How can we protect children's developmental needs while respecting commercial speech rights? What role should parents, educators, and regulators play in mediating children's exposure to advertising? And how can we create a media environment that supports children's healthy development in an increasingly commercialized world?

9. The Future of Advertising: Trends and Ethical Horizons

As technology advances and societal attitudes evolve, the landscape of advertising continues to transform. This section explores emerging trends in advertising and the new ethical challenges they present.

Emerging Trends:

1. Artificial Intelligence and Machine Learning:

   - Hyper-personalized ad experiences.

- AI-generated ad content.

- Predictive analytics for consumer behavior.

2. Virtual and Augmented Reality:

   - Immersive Brand experiences.

   - Virtual product try-ons and demonstrations.

   - AR-enhanced outdoor advertising.

3. Voice-Activated Advertising:

   - Integration of ads into voice assistant responses.

   - Voice-optimized search advertising.

4. Internet of Things (IoT) Advertising:

   - Ads delivered through smart home devices.

   - Location-based advertising via connected vehicles.

5. Neurotechnology in Advertising:

   - Brain-computer interfaces for ad interaction.

   - Neurometrics to measure ad effectiveness.

6. Blockchain in Advertising:

   - Transparent ad buying and selling processes.

   - Decentralized social media platforms with new ad models.

7. Sustainability-Focused Advertising:

   - Emphasis on eco-friendly products and practices.

   - Carbon footprint labeling in ads.

8. Post-Cookie Targeting:

- New methods of tracking and targeting as third-party cookies phase out.

- First-party data strategies.

9. Emotional AI:

- Ads that adapt based on detected emotional states.

- Mood-based targeting.

10. Quantum Computing:

- Ultra-complex modeling of consumer behavior.

- Quantum-enhanced optimization of ad placements.

Ethical Challenges and Considerations:

1. Privacy and Data Use:

- Balancing personalization with privacy protection.

- Ethical use of biometric and neurological data.

2. Transparency and Disclosure:

- Clearly identifying AI-generated content.

- Disclosure of emotional manipulation techniques.

3. Autonomy and Free Will:

- Protecting consumer choice in hyper-personalized ad environments.

- Addressing concerns about subliminal influence through advanced technologies.

4. Digital Divide:

- Ensuring equitable access to information in tech-driven ad landscapes.

- Avoiding discrimination in AI-powered ad targeting.

5. Mental Health:

- Impact of immersive and pervasive advertising on psychological well-being.

- Addressing potential addictive behaviors encouraged by new ad technologies.

6. Reality vs. Virtual Experience:

- Ethical implications of blurring lines between reality and advertising in VR/AR.

7. Child Protection:

- Safeguarding children in IoT and voice-activated ad environments.

- Regulating child-targeted content in immersive technologies.

8. Environmental Impact:

- Balancing technological advancement with sustainability concerns.

- Responsibility in promoting consumption through advanced ad techniques.

9. Global Governance:

- Developing international standards for emerging ad technologies.

- Addressing cultural differences in acceptance of new ad methods.

10. Human-AI Interaction:

- Defining ethical boundaries in human-AI relationships in advertising contexts.

Potential Ethical Frameworks and Approaches:

1. Ethics by Design: Integrating ethical considerations into the development of new advertising technologies.

2. Participatory Foresight: Involving diverse stakeholders in anticipating and shaping the future of advertising.

3. Adaptive Regulation: Developing flexible regulatory frameworks that can keep pace with technological change.

4. Digital Literacy Initiatives: Empowering consumers to navigate increasingly complex advertising landscapes.

5. Ethical AI Principles: Establishing guidelines for the development and use of AI in advertising.

Case Studies for the Future:

1. Neuro-Adaptive Billboards: Ethical implications of outdoor ads that change based on passersby's detected emotions.

2. Virtual Influencers: Navigating disclosure and authenticity with AI-generated brand ambassadors.

3. Predictive Purchase Ads: Ethical considerations of ads that anticipate and influence future buying decisions.

As we look to the future of advertising, key questions

emerge: How can we harness the potential of new technologies to create more relevant and valuable advertising experiences while respecting individual rights and societal well-being? What new skills and literacies will consumers need to navigate increasingly sophisticated advertising environments? And how can we create ethical frameworks that are robust enough to guide us through rapid technological change while remaining flexible enough to adapt to unforeseen developments?

10. Conclusion: Towards Ethical and Effective Advertising

As we conclude our exploration of advertising and its impact on the ego, we find ourselves at a critical juncture. Advertising, as a powerful force shaping individual psyches and societal values, carries both immense potential and significant responsibility.

Recap of Key Themes:

1. The psychological tactics used in advertising to influence consumer behavior and self-perception.

2. The evolving landscape of digital advertising and its implications for privacy and autonomy.

3. The role of advertising in shaping cultural values and norms.

4. The particular challenges and ethical considerations in advertising to children.

5. The future trends in advertising technology and their potential impacts.

<u>Moving forward, several key principles might guide our approach to more ethical and effective advertising:</u>

1. Transparency and Honesty: Ensuring that advertising is clearly identifiable and truthful in its claims.

2. Respect for Autonomy: Crafting advertising that informs and persuades without manipulating or exploiting psychological vulnerabilities.

3. Social Responsibility: Recognizing the power of advertising to shape culture and using this power to promote positive societal values.

4. Inclusivity and Representation: Ensuring diverse and respectful representation in advertising content.

5. Environmental Stewardship: Promoting sustainable consumption patterns and being mindful of the environmental impact of advertising practices.

6. Child Protection: Implementing strong safeguards to protect children from exploitative or harmful advertising.

7. Data Ethics: Using personal data for targeting and personalization in ways that respect privacy and informed consent.

8. Cultural Sensitivity: Creating advertising that respects and celebrates cultural differences rather than promoting a homogenized global culture.

9. Emotional Well-being: Considering the cumulative psychological impact of advertising on individual and societal mental health.

10. Technological Ethics: Developing and using new advertising technologies in ways that enhance rather than diminish human agency and well-being.

The path forward will require ongoing dialogue and

collaboration between advertisers, regulators, ethicists, and consumers. It will involve balancing commercial interests with social responsibility, creativity with truthfulness, and technological innovation with human values.

This may involve exploring new business models that align profit motives more closely with social good, developing more sophisticated regulatory frameworks that can keep pace with technological change, and fostering a culture of ethical advertising that goes beyond mere compliance to embrace a genuine commitment to societal well-being.

Education will play a crucial role in this transformation. We need to enhance media literacy at all levels of society, empowering consumers to critically engage with advertising messages and make informed choices. This education should extend to advertisers themselves, with a greater emphasis on ethics and social responsibility in marketing curricula and professional development.

As we navigate the future of advertising, we must also remain mindful of the broader context in which advertising operates. In a world facing pressing challenges such as climate change, social inequality, and political polarization, the power of advertising to shape attitudes and behaviors takes on added significance. Advertisers have the potential to be powerful allies in addressing these global issues, but this requires a fundamental shift in how we conceive of the purpose and responsibilities of advertising.

Moreover, as we grapple with the ethical implications of advertising, we have an opportunity to reflect more deeply on our values as a society. What do we truly value beyond material consumption? How do we define success and well-being? How can we foster a culture that prioritizes genuine human connection, creativity, and sustainability over endless acquisition?

The future of advertising also invites us to reconsider our understanding of the self and the ego. In a world where our identities are increasingly shaped by and expressed through consumption choices, how do we maintain a sense of authentic selfhood? How can we nurture healthier relationships with our own egos, less driven by comparison and external validation?

As we look to the future, it's clear that advertising will continue to be a significant force in our lives and societies. The choices we make now about how to shape and regulate this force will have profound implications for future generations. By approaching these choices with wisdom, ethical commitment, and a long-term perspective, we can work towards a future where advertising serves as a force for positive change rather than manipulation or exploitation.

In this endeavour, we might draw inspiration from various ethical and philosophical traditions. The emphasis on harmony and balance found in many Eastern philosophies could inform more holistic approaches to advertising that consider its wider impacts. The concept of "ubuntu" from African philosophy, which emphasizes our interconnectedness and mutual responsibility, could guide more community-oriented advertising practices. Western philosophical traditions of individual rights and social contract theory can help us navigate questions of autonomy and societal good in advertising.

Biblical wisdom, too, offers relevant insights. The injunction to "love your neighbour as yourself" (Leviticus 19:18) provides an ethical foundation that transcends mere commercial interests. The warning against covetousness found in the Ten Commandments speaks to the potential dangers of advertising that fosters endless desire for material goods. At the same time, parables about stewardship and the proper use of talents could inform discussions about the responsible use of advertising's persuasive power.

The future of advertising and its relationship to the ego is not predetermined. It will be shaped by the choices we make as creators, consumers, and regulators of advertising. By fostering critical awareness, ethical commitment, and a sense of shared responsibility, we can work towards a future where advertising enhances rather than diminishes our individual and collective well-being.

As we move forward, let us carry with us a vision of advertising that respects human dignity, fosters genuine connection, and contributes to the flourishing of all. In doing so, we can transform advertising from a potential source of manipulation and discontent into a powerful tool for positive social change and human development.

The journey towards more ethical and effective advertising is not an easy one. It requires us to question deeply ingrained practices, resist short-term profit motivations, and imagine new ways of communicating commercial messages. But in embarking on this journey, we create the potential for a media landscape that truly serves humanity – one that informs, inspires, and uplifts, rather than manipulates or exploits.

As we conclude, let us remember that every advertisement, marketing campaign, and brand message is an opportunity to respect human dignity, foster genuine value, and contribute to a more just and sustainable world. The power of advertising to shape egos and society is immense. Our collective responsibility is to ensure that this power is wielded wisely and ethically for the benefit of all.

CHAPTER 8:
PROPHECIES AND
WARNINGS

1. Introduction: The Timeless Voice of Prophecy

Throughout human history, prophecies and warnings have played a crucial role in shaping societies, guiding moral behaviour, and preparing people for potential future events. From ancient religious texts to modern-day futurists, the human desire to peer into the future and heed cautionary tales has been a constant across cultures and epochs.

This chapter will explore the nature of prophecy and warning, examining their historical significance, psychological impact, and relevance in our modern world. We will delve into various prophetic traditions, focusing on biblical prophecies, and consider how these ancient words might offer insight into contemporary challenges.

Our exploration will encompass:

1. The nature and purpose of prophecy

2. Biblical prophecies and their interpretations

3. Prophetic themes in other religious and cultural traditions

4. Modern-day prophecies and futurism

5. The psychology of prophecy and warning

6. Ethical considerations in interpreting and applying prophetic messages

7. The role of prophecy in shaping societal values and behaviours

8. Prophecy in the age of science and technology

9. The future of prophecy in a rapidly changing world

As we navigate this complex topic, we'll consider how prophetic messages intersect with current global issues such as environmental crises, technological advancements, social upheavals, and ethical dilemmas. We will examine how ancient warnings might guide addressing modern challenges while critically assessing prophetic interpretation's limitations and potential misuses.

We will balance respect for spiritual traditions with critical analytical thinking throughout our discussion. Our goal is not to predict the future or advocate for any particular prophetic interpretation but to understand the enduring human impulse toward prophecy and consider how prophetic wisdom might inform our approach to contemporary challenges.

By exploring the realm of prophecy and warning, we hope to gain insights into human nature, our relationship with the future, and our capacity for foresight and ethical action in the face of uncertainty.

2. The Nature and Purpose of Prophecy

Prophecy, in its broadest sense, refers to communicating divine or inspired messages, often about future events or moral imperatives. To understand prophecy's role in human society, it's crucial to explore its nature, functions, and the various forms it has taken across cultures and periods.

Key Aspects of Prophecy:

1. <u>Divine or Inspired Origin:</u>

  - Most prophetic traditions claim a supernatural or transcendent source for their messages.

  - This divine origin lends authority and urgency to prophetic utterances.

2. <u>Future-Oriented:</u>

  - While not all prophecies predict future events, many offer visions of what will come.

  - These can range from specific predictions to more general forecasts of trends or consequences.

3. <u>Moral and Ethical Dimension:</u>

  - Prophecies often include calls for moral reform or warnings about the consequences of unethical behaviour.

  - They frequently address societal issues and call for collective change.

4. <u>Symbolic and Metaphorical Language:</u>

  - Prophetic messages are often conveyed through rich symbolism and metaphor.

  - This can make interpretation challenging but allows for deeper, multi-layered meanings.

5. <u>Contextual Nature:</u>

- Prophecies are typically rooted in their origin's historical and cultural context.

- Understanding this context is crucial for interpretation.

Functions of Prophecy in Society:

1. <u>Guidance and Direction:</u>

- Prophecies can provide a sense of purpose and direction for individuals and communities.

- They often offer hope in times of uncertainty or crisis.

2. <u>Warning and Admonition:</u>

- Many prophecies serve as cautionary tales, warning of the potential consequences of current actions.

- This can motivate behavioural change and societal reform.

3. <u>Comfort and Reassurance:</u>

- Prophetic messages can offer comfort by promising ultimate justice or divine intervention.

- They can provide a sense of order and meaning in a chaotic world.

4. <u>Social Critique:</u>

- Prophets often serve as social critics, challenging the status quo and calling out injustice.

- This can be a catalyst for social change and reform.

5. <u>Identity Formation:</u>

- Prophetic traditions can be crucial in shaping group identity and cohesion.

- They provide a shared narrative and set of values for communities.

6. <u>Coping with Uncertainty:</u>

   - Prophecies can help people make sense of uncertain or challenging times.

   - They offer a framework for understanding and responding to change.

Types of Prophecy:

1. <u>Eschatological Prophecies:</u> Dealing with end times or the ultimate destiny of humanity.

2. <u>Messianic Prophecies:</u> Predicting the coming of a saviour or liberator figure.

3. <u>Social Justice Prophecies:</u> Focusing on societal reform and ethical behaviour.

4. <u>Personal Prophecies:</u> Directed at individuals, often about their life path or choices.

5. <u>National or Political Prophecies:</u> Concerning the fate of nations or political entities.

6. <u>Natural Disaster Prophecies:</u> Predicting environmental or cosmic events.

Challenges in Understanding Prophecy:

1. <u>Interpretation:</u> The often-symbolic nature of prophecy can lead to multiple, sometimes conflicting interpretations.

2. <u>Time Frame:</u> Many prophecies require clear time frames, making it difficult to assess their fulfilment.

3. <u>Cultural Translation:</u> Applying ancient prophecies to modern contexts requires careful consideration of cultural differences.

4. <u>Confirmation Bias:</u> People tend to see the fulfilment of prophecies in current events, potentially leading to forced interpretations.

5. <u>Ethical Implications:</u> How prophecies are interpreted and applied can have significant real-world consequences.

As we consider the nature and purpose of prophecy, key questions emerge: How can we responsibly interpret and apply prophetic messages in our modern context? What role should prophecy play in shaping individual and societal decision-making? And how do we balance respect for prophetic traditions with critical thinking and scientific understanding?

3. Biblical Prophecies: Themes and Interpretations

The Bible contains a rich tapestry of prophetic literature spanning the Old and New Testaments. These prophecies have profoundly impacted Western civilisation and continue to influence religious and cultural thought today. This section will explore some significant themes and interpretations of biblical prophecy.

Major Prophetic Books and Figures:

1. <u>Old Testament:</u>

   - Major Prophets: Isaiah, Jeremiah, Ezekiel, Daniel

   - Minor Prophets: Hosea, Joel, Amos, Obadiah, Jonah, Micah, Nahum, Habakkuk, Zephaniah, Haggai, Zechariah, Malachi

2. <u>New Testament:</u>

- Jesus Christ (as depicted in the Gospels)

- Book of Revelation

Key Themes in Biblical Prophecy:

1. <u>Covenant and Judgment:</u>

   - The concept of a divine covenant between God and His people

   - Warnings of judgment for breaking the covenant

   - Promises of restoration upon repentance

2. <u>Social Justice:</u>

   - Calls for fair treatment of the poor and marginalised

   - Condemnation of corruption and abuse of power

   - Emphasis on ethical behaviour in social and economic realms

3. <u>Messianic Prophecies:</u>

   - Predictions of a coming Messiah or Saviour figure

   - In Christianity, these are often interpreted as referring to Jesus Christ

4. <u>End Times (Eschatology):</u>

   - Visions of the "Day of the Lord" or final judgment

   - Descriptions of a new heaven and new earth

   - Concepts of resurrection and afterlife

5. <u>Restoration and Hope:</u>

- Promises of eventual redemption and restoration

- Visions of a peaceful future kingdom

6. <u>Universal Themes:</u>

- Prophecies extending beyond Israel to encompass all nations

- Messages of universal peace and justice

Interpretative Approaches:

1. <u>Literal Interpretation:</u>

- Taking prophetic texts at face value

- Often associated with fundamentalist or conservative approaches

2. <u>Allegorical Interpretation:</u>

- Viewing prophecies as symbolic representations of spiritual truths

- Common in more liberal or mystical traditions

3. <u>Historical-Critical Method:</u>

- Analysing prophecies in light of their historical and cultural context

- Emphasizes understanding the original meaning and audience

4. <u>Typological Interpretation:</u>

- Seeing Old Testament events and figures as "types" or foreshadowing of New Testament realities

- Common in Christian interpretations

5. <u>Preterist Approach:</u>

   - Viewing many prophecies as already fulfilled in the past

   - Often applied to apocalyptic literature like the Book of Revelation

6. <u>Futurist Approach:</u>

   - Interpreting prophecies as primarily referring to future events

   - Popular in some evangelical and dispensationalist circles

7. <u>Idealist Approach:</u>

   - Seeing prophecies as being timeless spiritual principles

   - Less concerned with specific historical fulfilments

Controversial Areas and Debates:

1. <u>End Times Scenarios:</u> Various interpretations of how and when biblical end-times prophecies will unfold.

2. <u>Prophecy and Modern Israel:</u> Debates over the role of modern Israel in biblical prophecy.

3. <u>Prophetic Time Frames:</u> There are discussions about whether prophetic "days" or "years" should be interpreted literally or symbolically.

4. <u>Messianic Prophecies:</u> Differences between Jewish and Christian interpretations of messianic texts.

5. <u>Prophecy and Science:</u> Attempts to reconcile prophetic visions with scientific understanding.

Ethical Considerations:

1. <u>Impact of Interpretations:</u> Different prophetic interpretations can influence political and social attitudes.

2. <u>Responsibility in Application:</u> The need for careful, contextual application of ancient prophecies to modern situations.

3. <u>Balancing Faith and Reason:</u> Navigating between religious belief and critical analysis in prophetic interpretation.

As we explore biblical prophecies, key questions arise: How can these ancient texts inform our understanding of current global challenges? What principles can we derive from prophetic literature to guide ethical decision-making today? And how do we responsibly interpret and apply biblical prophecies in a diverse, multi-faith world?

4. Prophetic Traditions in World Religions and Cultures

While our focus has been on biblical prophecy, we must recognise that prophetic traditions exist in many world religions and cultures. This section explores some of these diverse prophetic voices and their impact on societies.

Islam:

1. <u>Prophetic Tradition:</u>

   - Muhammad as the seal of the prophets

   - Hadith literature containing prophetic sayings and actions

2. <u>Key Themes:</u>

   - Day of Judgment (Yawm al-Qiyamah)

   - Signs of the Hour (portents of the end times)

- The coming of the Mahdi (guided one) and the return of Jesus

3. <u>Influential Figures:</u>

- Various Sufi mystics and scholars who made prophecies

Hinduism:

1. <u>Cyclical Time Concept:</u>

- Prophecies often relate to the cycle of yugas (ages)

2. <u>Key Themes:</u>

- Predictions about the Kali Yuga (current age of strife)

- Prophecies of avatar figures (divine incarnations)

3. <u>Texts:</u>

- Puranas contain many prophetic elements

- Bhavishya Purana specifically focused on future events

Buddhism:

1. <u>Prophetic Elements:</u>

- Predictions about the decline and eventual disappearance of the dharma

- Prophecies about future Buddhas, particularly Maitreya

2. <u>Texts:</u>

- Various sutras contain prophetic passages

- Kalachakra Tantra includes complex prophetic and cosmological ideas

Native American Traditions:

1. <u>Diverse Prophetic Voices:</u>

   - Varied across different tribes and cultures

2. <u>Notable Examples:</u>

   - Hopi prophecies about world ages and environmental changes

   - Lakota White Buffalo Calf Woman prophecies

3. <u>Themes:</u>

   - Often focused on harmony with nature and warnings about departure from traditional ways

African Traditional Religions:

1. <u>Divination Practices:</u>

   - Many cultures have systems of foretelling future events

2. <u>Prophetic Figures:</u>

   - Various tribal prophets and seers

   - Example: Nongqawuse in Xhosa history

Chinese Traditions:

1. <u>I Ching (Book of Changes):</u>

   - Ancient text used for divination and understanding future trends

2. <u>Taoist Prophecies:</u>

   - Predictions about cosmic cycles and human society

Ancient Greek and Roman Traditions:

1. <u>Oracles:</u>

   - Such as the Oracle of Delphi

2. <u>Sibylline Books:</u>

   - Prophetic texts consulted by Roman authorities

Modern Spiritual Movements:

1. <u>New Age Prophecies:</u>

   - Often blending elements from various traditions

   - Focus on personal transformation and global shift in consciousness

2. <u>Spiritualist Movements:</u>

   - Channeling of prophetic messages from spirits or ascended masters

Comparative Themes:

1. <u>Cyclical Time:</u>

   - Many traditions view time as cyclical rather than linear

2. <u>Golden Age Myths:</u>

   - Prophecies of a return to an idealised past or the dawn of a new golden age

3. <u>Apocalyptic Visions:</u>

   - End-time scenarios are common across many cultures

4. <u>Environmental Warnings:</u>

- Many traditions include prophecies about humanity's relationship with nature

5. <u>Messianic Figures:</u>

- Predictions of saviour or enlightened leader figures are widespread

6. <u>Moral and Ethical Focus:</u>

- Prophecies often emphasise the need for moral reform and ethical living

Challenges in Cross-Cultural Prophetic Study:

1. <u>Cultural Context:</u> Understanding prophecies within their original cultural frameworks

2. <u>Translation Issues:</u> Accurately conveying prophetic concepts across languages

3. <u>Syncretism:</u> Recognizing where prophetic traditions have influenced each other

4. <u>Universality vs. Particularity:</u> Balancing universal themes with culture-specific elements

Ethical Considerations:

1. <u>Respect for Diverse Traditions:</u> Approaching different prophetic traditions with cultural sensitivity

2. <u>Comparative Analysis:</u> Finding common ground while respecting unique elements of each tradition

3. <u>Modern Application:</u> Responsibly applying ancient wisdom to contemporary challenges

4. <u>Interfaith Dialogue:</u> Using prophetic traditions as a basis for

cross-cultural understanding

As we explore these diverse prophetic traditions, key questions emerge: What universal human needs and concerns are reflected in prophecies across cultures? How can studying varied prophetic traditions enhance our understanding of human spirituality and foresight? And how might these diverse voices contribute to addressing global challenges in our interconnected world?

5. Modern Prophecies and Futurism

While traditional religious prophecies continue to influence many, new forms of prediction and foresight have emerged in the modern era. This section explores contemporary approaches to prophecy, from secular futurism to modern spiritual movements.

Secular Futurism:

1. <u>Scientific Predictions:</u>

   - Climate change models and environmental forecasts

   - Technological singularity theories

   - Demographic and sociological projections

2. <u>Trend Analysis:</u>

   - Economic forecasting

   - Geopolitical analysis and scenario planning

   - Social trend prediction

3. <u>Futurology as an Academic Discipline:</u>

   - Study of possible, probable, and preferable futures

- Use of methods like Delphi technique and cross-impact analysis

4. <u>Transhumanism:</u>

   - Predictions about human enhancement and technological integration

   - Visions of post-human futures

5. <u>Artificial Intelligence Predictions:</u>

   - Forecasts about the development and impact of AI

   - Scenarios ranging from utopian to existential risk

Modern Spiritual and New Age Prophecies:

1. <u>Channeled Messages:</u>

   - Claims of communication with extraterrestrial or interdimensional beings

   - Messages from ascended masters or spirit guides

2. <u>Earth Changes Prophecies:</u>

   - Predictions of geological and climatic shifts

   - Often blending scientific data with spiritual interpretations

3. <u>Consciousness Shift Theories:</u>

   - Prophecies about global awakening or shift in human consciousness

   - Concepts like the "Hundredth Monkey Effect"

4. <u>Reinterpretations of Ancient Prophecies:</u>

- Modern readings of Mayan calendar end-date

- New interpretations of Nostradamus or biblical prophecies

5. <u>Psychic Predictions:</u>

- Individual psychics making public predictions about world events

- Often annual predictions about celebrities, politics, and natural disasters

Contemporary Religious Prophecy:

1. <u>Modern Christian Prophetic Movements:</u>

- Charismatic and Pentecostal prophetic practices

- Interpretations of biblical prophecy in light of current events

2. <u>Islamic Eschatological Movements:</u>

- Contemporary interpretations of end-times hadith

- Mahdi movements

3. <u>New Religious Movements:</u>

- Prophetic elements in groups like Scientology or Raëlism

4. <u>Apocalyptic Cults:</u>

- Groups formed around specific end-times predictions

- Often with tragic consequences (e.g., Heaven's Gate)

Technological Tools for Prediction:

1. <u>Big Data Analysis:</u>

- Using vast datasets to name patterns and make predictions

2. <u>Predictive Algorithms:</u>

- AI and machine learning used for various forms of forecasting

3. <u>Simulation and Modelling:</u>

- Computer models used to simulate complex systems and potential futures

4. <u>Social Media Analysis:</u>

- Using social media trends to predict societal shifts and behaviours

5. <u>Quantum Computing:</u>

- Potential future applications in complex predictive modelling

Challenges in Modern Prophecy and Futurism:

1. <u>Information Overload:</u>

- Abundance of predictions and forecasts can lead to confusion or apathy

2. <u>Rapid Pace of Change:</u>

- Accelerating technological and social change makes long-term prediction difficult

3. <u>Complexity and Interconnectedness:</u>

- Global systems are increasingly complex, making linear predictions less reliable

4. <u>Bias and Assumptions:</u>

- Personal, cultural, and technological biases can skew predictions

5. <u>Self-Fulfilling or Self-Defeating Prophecies:</u>

- Predictions can influence behaviour, potentially altering the predicted outcome

6. <u>Ethical Implications:</u>

- Predictions can have real-world consequences, raising questions of responsibility

7. <u>Distinguishing Signal from Noise:</u>

- Separating meaningful trends from random fluctuations or misinformation

Ethical Considerations in Modern Prophecy:

1. <u>Responsibility in Prediction:</u>

- Balancing the desire to warn or prepare with the potential for causing undue alarm

2. <u>Transparency in Methods:</u>

- Communicating the basis and limitations of predictions

3. <u>Handling Uncertainty:</u>

- Ethically presenting probabilities and ranges of possible futures

4. <u>Impact on Decision Making:</u>

- Understanding how predictions influence policy, investment, and personal choices

5. <u>Accessibility and Equality:</u>

- Ensuring that predictive insights are not limited to only the wealthy or powerful

6. <u>Privacy Concerns:</u>

- Ethical use of personal data in predictive analytics

As we consider modern prophecies and futurism, key questions emerge: How can we responsibly use predictive technologies and insights to shape a better future? What is the appropriate balance between heeding warnings and maintaining optimism about the future? And how do we navigate the ethical challenges of increasingly powerful predictive capabilities?

6. The Psychology of Prophecy and Warning

Understanding the psychological aspects of prophecy and warning is crucial for grasping their enduring appeal and impact on human behaviour. This section explores the cognitive, emotional, and social-psychological factors influencing people's engagement with prophetic messages.

Cognitive Factors:

1. <u>Pattern Recognition:</u>

- Human tendency to seek patterns, sometimes leading to seeing prophetic fulfilment where none exists

- Pareidolia in prophetic interpretation

2. <u>Confirmation Bias:</u>

- Tendency to focus on information that confirms pre-existing beliefs about prophecies

- Ignoring or rationalising away disconfirming evidence

3. <u>Anchoring Effect:</u>

- Initial exposure to a prophecy can strongly influence subsequent interpretations of events

4. <u>Availability Heuristic:</u>

- Recent or vivid events may be seen as more prophetically significant than they are

5. <u>Cognitive Dissonance:</u>

- Mental discomfort when prophecies fail, often leading to rationalisation or reinterpretation

Emotional Factors:

1. <u>Fear and Anxiety:</u>

- Prophecies, especially those of doom, can trigger deep-seated fears

- Anxiety about the future can increase receptivity to prophetic messages

2. <u>Hope and Optimism:</u>

- Positive prophecies can provide comfort and motivation

- Belief in a prophesied better future can inspire action

3. <u>Sense of Control:</u>

- Prophecies can offer a sense of control or understanding in chaotic times

- Illusion of predictability in an unpredictable world

4. <u>Awe and Wonder:</u>

- Prophetic experiences or interpretations can evoke feelings of transcendence

- Sense of connection to something greater than oneself

Social Psychological Factors:

1. <u>Group Identity:</u>

- Shared belief in prophecies can strengthen group cohesion

- Prophecies often reinforce in-group/out-group distinctions

2. <u>Authority and Credibility:</u>

- Perception of prophetic figures as authorities can lead to uncritical acceptance

- Credibility heuristics in assessing prophetic claims

3. <u>Social Proof:</u>

- Witnessing others' belief in prophecies can increase one's own belief

- Role of social media in amplifying prophetic messages

4. <u>Narrative Psychology:</u>

- Prophecies often fit into broader cultural narratives or personal life stories

- Power of prophetic narratives in meaning-making

5. <u>Terror Management Theory:</u>

- Prophecies, especially religious ones, can serve as a buffer against existential anxiety

Psychological Functions of Prophecy:

1. <u>Coping Mechanism:</u>

   - Prophecies can help people cope with uncertainty and fear of the unknown

2. <u>Meaning and Purpose:</u>

   - Prophetic beliefs can provide a sense of meaning and purpose in life

3. <u>Moral Guidance:</u>

   - Prophecies often include ethical directives, shaping behaviour

4. <u>Identity Formation:</u>

   - Belief in specific prophecies can be a key part of personal or group identity

5. <u>Motivation for Change:</u>

   - Prophecies of doom can motivate behavioural or societal changes

Psychological Impacts of Failed Prophecies:

1. <u>Cognitive Dissonance Resolution:</u>

   - Various strategies used to resolve the discomfort of unfulfilled prophecies

2. <u>Strengthening of Beliefs:</u>

   - Paradoxical reinforcement of beliefs in some cases of prophetic failure

3. <u>Disillusionment and Loss of Faith:</u>

   - Potential for significant psychological distress when firmly held prophetic beliefs are disconfirmed

4. <u>Shifting Goalposts:</u>

   - Tendency to reinterpret or reschedule failed prophecies

Ethical Considerations in the Psychology of Prophecy:

1. <u>Vulnerability to Manipulation:</u>

   - Understanding how psychological factors can be exploited in spreading prophetic messages

2. <u>Mental Health Impacts:</u>

   - Balancing potential positive psychological effects with risks of anxiety or delusion

3. <u>Responsible Communication:</u>

   - Ethical considerations in how prophetic or predictive information is presented

4. <u>Critical Thinking:</u>

   - Importance of fostering critical thinking skills to evaluate prophetic claims

As we explore the psychology of prophecy and warning, key questions arise: How can we harness the positive psychological aspects of prophecy while mitigating potential negative impacts? What role does understanding the psychology of prophecy play in interpreting and applying prophetic messages responsibly? And how can this knowledge inform our approach to modern challenges and decision-making in an uncertain world?

7. Prophecy and Social Change: Catalysts for Transformation

Throughout history, prophecies have often served as powerful catalysts for social change. This section explores how prophetic messages have influenced societal transformations and considers their potential role in addressing contemporary global challenges.

Historical Examples of Prophecy-Driven Change:

1. <u>Abolitionist Movement:</u>

   - Religious prophecies and visions playing a role in motivating anti-slavery activists

2. <u>Civil Rights Movement:</u>

   - Prophetic tradition in African American churches inspiring and sustaining the movement

3. <u>Environmental Awareness:</u>

   - Native American prophecies contributing to modern environmental consciousness

4. <u>Women's Suffrage:</u>

   - Religious and spiritual visions motivating early feminists

5. <u>Anti-Apartheid Movement:</u>

   - Prophetic elements in religious opposition to apartheid in South Africa

Mechanisms of Prophetic Influence on Society:

1. <u>Moral Framing:</u>

   - Prophecies providing ethical frameworks for social issues

2. <u>Visionary Leadership:</u>

- Prophetic figures often emerging as charismatic leaders of social movements

3. <u>Collective Action:</u>

- Shared prophetic beliefs mobilising groups towards common goals

4. <u>Cultural Critique:</u>

- Prophetic messages challenging existing social norms and power structures

5. <u>Hope and Empowerment:</u>

- Positive prophecies inspiring belief in the possibility of change

6. <u>Urgency and Motivation:</u>

- Apocalyptic prophecies creating a sense of urgency for reform

Contemporary Applications:

1. <u>Climate Change Activism:</u>

- Prophetic-style warnings from scientists and activists mobilising environmental movements

2. <u>Social Justice Movements:</u>

- Prophetic rhetoric in movements like Black Lives Matter or Me Too

3. <u>Technological Ethics:</u>

- Cautionary "prophecies" about AI and biotechnology shaping ethical debates

4. <u>Economic Reform:</u>

- Prophetic critiques of capitalism influencing movements for economic justice

5. <u>Peace and Conflict Resolution:</u>

- Prophetic visions of peace inspiring diplomatic and grassroots peace efforts

Challenges in Prophecy-Driven Social Change:

1. <u>Interpretation Debates:</u>

- Conflicts over the meaning and application of prophetic messages

2. <u>Resistance to Change:</u>

- Established powers often resisting prophetically-inspired reforms

3. <u>Balancing Urgency and Pragmatism:</u>

- Navigating between prophetic idealism and practical, incremental change

4. <u>Potential for Extremism:</u>

- Risk of prophecy-inspired movements becoming radicalised

5. <u>Credibility and Evidence:</u>

- Maintaining credibility when prophetic claims conflict with scientific or historical evidence

Ethical Considerations:

1. <u>Responsible Activism:</u>

- Using prophetic messages to inspire positive change without manipulation

2. <u>Inclusivity:</u>

- Ensuring prophecy-inspired movements are inclusive and respectful of diversity

3. <u>Accountability:</u>

- Holding prophetic leaders and movements accountable for their claims and actions

4. <u>Balancing Tradition and Progress:</u>

- Reconciling traditional prophetic wisdom with modern scientific and social understanding

5. <u>Global Impact:</u>

- Considering the worldwide implications of prophecy-driven social movements in an interconnected world

Future Potential:

1. <u>Global Cooperation:</u>

- Prophetic visions of unity potentially inspiring international collaboration on global challenges

2. <u>Sustainable Development:</u>

- Prophetic ecological wisdom informing sustainable development practices

3. <u>Technological Stewardship:</u>

- Prophetic cautions guiding responsible development of emerging technologies

4. <u>Cultural Renewal:</u>

- Prophecy-inspired movements contributing to cultural and spiritual revitalisation

5. <u>Conflict Transformation:</u>

- Prophetic peace traditions informing new approaches to conflict resolution

As we consider the role of prophecy in social change, key questions emerge: How can prophetic traditions constructively inform our response to current global challenges? What is the appropriate balance between prophetic vision and practical policy-making? And how can we ensure that prophecy-inspired social movements contribute positively to human progress and well-being?

8. Prophecy in the Age of Science and Technology

The role and nature of prophecy have evolved in an era dominated by scientific understanding and technological advancement. This section explores the intersection of traditional prophetic thinking and modern scientific and technological developments.

Challenges to Traditional Prophecy:

1. <u>Scientific Method:</u>

- Emphasis on empirical evidence and falsifiability challenging prophetic claims

2. <u>Technological Prediction:</u>

- Advanced forecasting tools competing with traditional prophetic methods

3. <u>Secularization:</u>

- Declining influence of religious institutions in many societies affecting reception of prophecies

4. <u>Information Access:</u>

- Widespread access to information making it harder for false prophecies to go unchallenged

5. <u>Complexity of Global Systems:</u>

- Interconnected nature of world systems complicating straightforward prophetic narratives

Convergences of Prophecy and Science:

1. <u>Climate Science:</u>

- Scientific climate predictions echoing themes from ancient environmental prophecies

2. <u>Existential Risk Studies:</u>

- Academic research on global catastrophic risks paralleling apocalyptic prophecies

3. <u>Neuroscience of Religious Experience:</u>

- Scientific study of prophetic experiences and visions

4. <u>Quantum Physics and Mysticism:</u>

- Some interpret quantum phenomena as validation of prophetic or mystical worldviews

5. <u>Artificial Intelligence:</u>

- some see AI prediction capabilities as a modern form of prophecy

Technological "Prophecy":

1. <u>Big Data Analytics:</u>

   - Using vast datasets to predict trends and events

2. <u>Predictive Algorithms:</u>

   - AI systems making forecasts in fields from weather to stock markets

3. <u>Scenario Planning:</u>

   - Corporate and governmental use of systematic future scenario development

4. <u>Digital Simulations:</u>

   - Complex computer models simulating potential future outcomes

5. <u>Internet of Things (IoT):</u>

   - Networked devices providing real-time data for predictive analysis

Ethical Considerations:

1. <u>Technological Determinism:</u>

   - Balancing belief in technological "prophecies" with human agency and ethics

2. <u>Data Privacy:</u>

   - Ethical use of personal data in predictive technologies

3. <u>Algorithmic Bias:</u>

   - Ensuring fairness and avoiding discrimination in AI-driven predictions

4. <u>Transparency:</u>

   - Making the basis of technological predictions understandable to the public

5. <u>Human-AI Collaboration:</u>

   - Determining the appropriate balance between human judgment and AI predictions

New Forms of "Prophetic" Voices:

1. <u>Science Communicators:</u>

   - Public figures translating complex scientific predictions for general audiences

2. <u>Tech Visionaries:</u>

   - Entrepreneurs and innovators making bold predictions about technological futures

3. <u>Futurists:</u>

   - Professional future scenario developers and trend analysts

4. <u>Online Influencers:</u>

   - Social media personalities shaping public perceptions of future trends

5. <u>Data Journalists:</u>

   - Reporters using data analysis to uncover and predict societal trends

Integrating Traditional and Modern Approaches:

1. <u>Ethical Frameworks:</u>

- Using traditional prophetic wisdom to inform ethical guidelines for new technologies

2. <u>Holistic Foresight:</u>

- Combining scientific prediction with insights from humanities and spirituality

3. <u>Narrative Power:</u>

- Utilizing the storytelling aspect of prophecy to communicate complex scientific concepts

4. <u>Collective Wisdom:</u>

- Integrating Indigenous and traditional knowledge with scientific understanding

5. <u>Mindfulness and Technology:</u>

- Applying contemplative practices to the development and use of predictive technologies

Future Directions:

1. <u>AI Ethics:</u>

- Potential for AI systems to incorporate ethical principles derived from prophetic traditions

2. <u>Virtual Reality Prophecy:</u>

- Use of VR to create immersive experiences of potential futures

3. <u>Citizen Science and Prophecy:</u>

- Crowdsourcing of data and insights for predictive models

4. <u>Neuro-ethics:</u>

- Exploring the ethical implications of potential future mind-enhancement technologies

5. <u>Space Exploration:</u>

   - How prophetic visions might inform or be challenged by discoveries in space

As we navigate the intersection of prophecy with science and technology, key questions arise: How can we integrate the wisdom of prophetic traditions with the insights of modern science? What new forms of "prophecy" might emerge from advancing technology, and how should we approach them ethically? And how can this integration contribute to addressing the complex challenges facing humanity in the 21st century and beyond?

9. The Future of Prophecy: Adapting Ancient Wisdom to Modern Challenges

As we look to the future, the role and nature of prophecy continue to evolve. This final section explores how prophetic traditions might adapt to address contemporary issues and what new forms of foresight might emerge.

Emerging Trends in Prophetic Thought:

1. <u>Ecological Prophecy:</u>

   - Integration of environmental science with traditional ecological wisdom

   - Prophetic voices calling for sustainable living and earth stewardship

2. <u>Technological Ethics:</u>

   - Prophetic warnings about the potential dangers of

unchecked technological advancement

- Visions of harmonious human-technology integration

3. <u>Global Unity:</u>

- Prophecies emphasising the interconnectedness of humanity

- Calls for international cooperation to address global challenges

4. <u>Consciousness Evolution:</u>

- Predictions of shifts in human consciousness and spiritual awakening

- Integration of neuroscience with spiritual practices

5. <u>Space Exploration:</u>

- Prophetic visions extending to humanity's future beyond Earth

- Ethical considerations for space colonisation and extraterrestrial contact

Adapting Prophetic Wisdom to Modern Contexts:

1. <u>Reinterpretation of Ancient Texts:</u>

- Reading traditional prophecies through the lens of contemporary issues

- Finding universal principles in specific cultural contexts

2. <u>Interfaith Dialogue:</u>

- Bringing together diverse prophetic traditions to address common concerns

- Creating syncretic approaches to global challenges

3. <u>Science-Spirituality Integration:</u>

- Finding common ground between scientific prediction and spiritual foresight

- Developing holistic approaches to understanding future possibilities

4. <u>Digital Prophecy:</u>

- Using social media and digital platforms to disseminate prophetic messages

- Crowdsourcing of prophetic insights and interpretations

5. <u>Ethical AI Development:</u>

- Incorporating prophetic wisdom into the development of artificial intelligence ethics

- Exploring the potential for AI to assist in processing and interpreting prophetic texts

Challenges and Ethical Considerations:

1. <u>Discernment:</u>

- Developing criteria to distinguish genuine insight from sensationalism or manipulation

2. <u>Cultural Sensitivity:</u>

- Respecting diverse cultural traditions while addressing universal human concerns

3. <u>Adaptability vs. Authenticity:</u>

- Balancing the need to adapt ancient wisdom with

maintaining its essence

4. <u>Prophecy and Policy:</u>

   - Ethically integrating prophetic insights into public policy and decision-making

5. <u>Individual vs. Collective:</u>

   - Navigating between personal spiritual experiences and collective prophetic narratives

6. <u>Technological Mediation:</u>

   - Considering how digital technologies might alter the nature of prophetic experiences and communication

Potential Future Forms of Prophecy:

1. <u>AI-Assisted Prophecy:</u>

   - Use of artificial intelligence to analyse patterns in religious texts

2. <u>Quantum Prophecy:</u>

   - Exploration of prophetic insights based on quantum physics principles

   - Potential for understanding multiple futures or parallel realities

3. <u>Neuro-Prophecy:</u>

   - Use of brain-computer interfaces to access altered states of consciousness

   - Scientific study of brain states associated with prophetic experiences

4. <u>Collective Intelligence Prophecy:</u>

- Harnessing the wisdom of crowds through advanced networking technologies

- Global collaborative efforts to envision and shape the future

5. <u>Biotech Prophecy:</u>

- Exploring the ethical and spiritual implications of human enhancement technologies

- Prophetic visions related to the future of human evolution

6. <u>Virtual Reality Prophecy:</u>

- Immersive experiences of potential futures or prophetic visions

- Use of VR for collective visioning exercises

7. <u>Eco-Systemic Prophecy:</u>

- Integrating insights from ecology, systems thinking, and traditional wisdom

- Holistic approaches to predicting and shaping planetary futures

8. <u>Space-Based Prophecy:</u>

- New perspectives on humanity's future derived from space exploration

- Potential for off-world prophetic experiences or insights

9. <u>Transhumanist Prophecy:</u>

- Visions of post-human futures and their ethical

implications

- Integrating traditional prophetic wisdom with futurist thought

10. <u>Interdimensional Prophecy:</u>

- Exploration of prophetic insights claiming to originate from other dimensions or realities

- Scientific investigation of claims of interdimensional communication

Ethical Framework for Future Prophecy:

1. <u>Transparency:</u>

- Clear communication about the sources and methods of prophetic insights

2. <u>Accountability:</u>

- Mechanisms for evaluating the impact and accuracy of prophetic claims

3. <u>Inclusivity:</u>

- Ensuring diverse voices and perspectives are included in prophetic dialogues

4. <u>Harm Reduction:</u>

- Prioritizing approaches that minimise potential negative psychological or social impacts

5. <u>Scientific Integrity:</u>

- Maintaining rigorous standards when integrating scientific methods with prophetic practices

6. <u>Spiritual Authenticity:</u>

   - Honoring the depth and sincerity of genuine spiritual experiences

7. <u>Global Responsibility:</u>

   - Considering the worldwide implications of prophetic messages and movements

8. <u>Ethical Use of Technology:</u>

   - Developing guidelines for the responsible use of advanced technologies in prophetic practices

Preparing for the Future of Prophecy:

1. <u>Education:</u>

   - Developing curricula that integrate critical thinking, spiritual wisdom, and futurist thought

2. <u>Interfaith and Interdisciplinary Collaboration:</u>

   - Creating forums for dialogue between religious leaders, scientists, and futurists

3. <u>Ethical Guidelines:</u>

   - Establishing flexible but robust ethical frameworks for new forms of prophetic practice

4. <u>Public Engagement:</u>

   - Fostering informed public discourse about the role of prophecy in modern society

5. <u>Technological Development:</u>

   - Ethical development of technologies that might enhance or

transform prophetic practices

6. <u>Preservation of Wisdom:</u>

   - Efforts to preserve and understand traditional prophetic texts and practices

7. <u>Adaptive Spirituality:</u>

   - Nurturing spiritual traditions that can evolve with changing knowledge and circumstances

As we contemplate the future of prophecy, key questions emerge: How can we honour ancient wisdom while embracing new insights and technologies? What role should prophetic thinking play in shaping our collective future? How do we balance openness to new forms of foresight with critical discernment? And how can prophetic wisdom contribute to addressing the complex, global challenges of the 21st century and beyond?

10. Conclusion: Integrating Prophecy and Warning in the Modern World

As we conclude our exploration of prophecies and warnings, we find ourselves at a crucial juncture where ancient wisdom intersects with modern challenges and technological advancements. The enduring human impulse to peer into the future and heed cautionary tales remains as relevant as ever, even as the forms and interpretations of prophecy evolve.

Recap of Key Themes:

1. The historical significance and psychological impact of prophecy across cultures

2. The role of biblical and other religious prophecies in shaping societal values and behaviours

3. The emergence of modern, secular forms of prediction and foresight

4. The psychological underpinnings of our engagement with prophetic messages

5. The potential of prophecy to catalyse social change and address global challenges

6. The intersection of traditional prophetic thinking with scientific and technological advancements

7. The evolving nature of prophecy in response to contemporary issues

Moving forward, several key principles might guide our approach to prophecy and warning in the modern world:

1. <u>Critical Discernment:</u> Developing the ability to evaluate prophetic claims while remaining open to genuine insights critically.

2. <u>Ethical Integration:</u> Incorporating the ethical wisdom found in prophetic traditions into our approach to modern challenges.

3. <u>Scientific Harmony:</u> Seeking ways to harmonise scientific understanding with the insights of prophetic traditions.

4. <u>Cultural Sensitivity:</u> Respecting the diversity of prophetic traditions while identifying universal themes and values.

5. <u>Technological Wisdom:</u> Applying prophetic caution and foresight to develop and use emerging technologies.

6. <u>Global Perspective:</u> Recognizing the interconnected nature of global challenges and the need for collective foresight.

7. <u>Psychological Awareness:</u> Understanding the psychological

impacts of prophetic messages and using this knowledge responsibly.

8. <u>Adaptive Interpretation:</u> Reinterpreting ancient prophecies in light of contemporary contexts while preserving their core wisdom.

9. <u>Inclusive Dialogue:</u> Fostering open conversations between diverse voices - religious leaders, scientists, futurists, and the public.

10. <u>Action Orientation:</u> Moving beyond mere prediction to inspired, ethical action in addressing global issues.

The future of prophecy and warning will likely involve a complex interplay of tradition and innovation. We may see new forms of "prophecy" emerge, powered by advanced technologies and collective intelligence. At the same time, ancient wisdom traditions will continue to offer valuable insights and ethical frameworks for navigating an uncertain future.

Prophetic thinking becomes increasingly crucial as we face unprecedented global challenges, from climate change and technological disruption to social inequalities and geopolitical tensions. It is not a means of predicting a fixed future but of envisioning possible futures and motivating wise action in the present.

In this context, prophecy can serve not just as a warning of potential dangers. Still, as a beacon of hope and a call to collective responsibility. It can inspire us to imagine and work towards more just, sustainable, and fulfilling futures for all humanity.

However, as we engage with prophetic messages and foresight, we must remain mindful of the ethical implications.

The power to shape perceptions of the future comes with great responsibility. We must strive for transparency, accountability, and inclusivity in our prophetic discourses and ensure they contribute to the greater good rather than exacerbate fears or divisions.

Education will play a crucial role in this future. We must foster a populace that can engage critically and creatively with ancient wisdom and cutting-edge foresight. This involves cultivating media literacy, critical thinking skills, ethical reasoning, and an appreciation for diverse perspectives.

As we navigate the complex landscape of modern prophecy and warning, we might draw inspiration from various spiritual and philosophical traditions. The emphasis on wisdom, compassion, and interconnectedness found in many of these traditions can provide valuable guidance as we face the challenges of our time.

Ultimately, the future of prophecy and warning is not predetermined. It will be shaped by how we engage with prophetic traditions, develop new forms of foresight, and apply these insights to the pressing issues of our day. By approaching this task with wisdom, ethical commitment, and a spirit of global cooperation, we can work towards a future where prophetic insight is a powerful tool for human flourishing and the betterment of our world.

As we conclude, let us remember that every engagement with prophecy and warning—whether ancient or modern—is an opportunity to reflect deeply on our values, place in the world, and responsibilities to each other and future generations. Prophecy's true power lies not in its ability to predict the future but in its capacity to inspire us to create a better one.

CHAPTER 9: THE WAY FORWARD

1. Introduction: Charting a Course Through Complexity

As we strive to conclude our exploration of the various facets of ego and arrogance and their manifestations in modern society, we find ourselves at a critical juncture. The challenges we face—from environmental crises to technological disruptions social inequalities to ethical dilemmas in healthcare and beyond—are complex and interconnected. Yet, within these challenges lie opportunities for transformation and growth, both as individuals and as a global community.

This closing chapter synthesises the insights gained from our previous discussions and charts a way forward. We will explore strategies for combating ego and arrogance at the individual and societal levels, drawing on biblical concepts of humility, community, servant leadership and contemporary understandings of psychology, sociology, and systems thinking.

Our journey through this chapter will encompass:

1. <u>Personal transformation</u>: Strategies for cultivating humility and self-awareness

2. <u>Interpersonal dynamics:</u> Fostering empathy and genuine connection

3. <u>Organizational change</u>: Reimagining leadership and institutional structures

4. <u>Societal shifts</u>: Addressing systemic issues and cultural narratives

5. <u>Global perspectives</u>: Navigating international challenges with wisdom and cooperation

6. <u>Technological ethics</u>: Ensuring human values guide our technological future

7. <u>Environmental stewardship</u>: Cultivating a sustainable relationship with our planet

8. <u>Education and lifelong learning</u>: Preparing for an uncertain future

9. <u>Spiritual and philosophical integration</u>: Finding meaning and purpose in a complex world

Throughout this chapter, we will strive to balance idealism with pragmatism, recognising that meaningful change often occurs through a combination of bold vision and incremental steps. We will also acknowledge the diversity of human experiences and perspectives, seeking common ground while respecting cultural differences.

By the end of this chapter, we aim to provide a roadmap - not a rigid plan, but a flexible framework - for navigating the challenges of our time with wisdom, compassion, and a sense of shared purpose. Our goal is to inspire hope and motivate action, recognising that the way forward, while not always straightforward, is one we must walk together.

2. Personal Transformation: The Foundation of Change

Personal transformation is central to addressing the

challenges posed by ego and arrogance. This section explores strategies for cultivating humility, self-awareness, and a more balanced sense of self.

Key Aspects of Personal Transformation:

1. <u>Self-Awareness:</u>

   - Developing the ability to observe one's thoughts, emotions, and behaviours objectively

   - Regular self-reflection practices such as journaling or meditation

   - Seeking feedback from others and being open to constructive criticism

2. <u>Emotional Intelligence:</u>

   - Cultivating the ability to recognise and manage one's own emotions

   - Developing empathy and the capacity to understand others' emotional states

   - Practicing emotional regulation techniques

3. <u>Mindfulness:</u>

   - Engaging in mindfulness practices to stay present and reduce ego-driven reactivity

   - Cultivating a non-judgmental awareness of one's experiences

   - Using mindfulness to create space between stimulus and response

4. <u>Cognitive Restructuring:</u>

- Identifying and challenging ego-driven thought patterns

- Developing more balanced and realistic self-assessments

- Practicing cognitive flexibility and openness to new perspectives

5. <u>Humility:</u>

- Cultivating a realistic view of one's strengths and limitations

- Developing a learning orientation and openness to growth

- Practicing gratitude and recognising one's interdependence with others

6. <u>Value Clarification:</u>

- Identifying core personal values beyond ego-driven desires

- Aligning daily actions with deeper values and principles

- Developing a sense of purpose beyond personal gain or status

7. <u>Compassion and Self-Compassion:</u>

- Cultivating kindness towards oneself and others

- Developing a balanced self-view that acknowledges both strengths and weaknesses

- Practicing forgiveness, both of oneself and others

Strategies for Personal Transformation:

1. <u>Mindfulness Meditation:</u>

- Regular practice of mindfulness to develop present-moment awareness

- Loving-kindness meditation to cultivate compassion

2. <u>Journaling:</u>

- Reflective writing to gain insights into thoughts and behaviours

- Gratitude journaling to foster appreciation and humility

3. <u>Therapy or Counseling:</u>

- Professional support in addressing deep-seated ego patterns

- Cognitive-behavioral therapy (CBT) for restructuring thought patterns

4. <u>Education and Reading:</u>

- Engaging with diverse perspectives through literature and philosophy

- Studying psychology and personal development

5. <u>Body-Mind Practices:</u>

- Yoga, tai chi, or other practices that integrate physical and mental awareness

- Breathwork techniques for emotional regulation

6. <u>Service and Volunteering:</u>

- Engaging in altruistic activities to shift focus beyond the self

- Developing empathy through direct engagement with others' needs

7. <u>Intentional Discomfort:</u>

- Purposefully engaging in challenging situations that push one out of the comfort zone

- Embracing failure as a learning opportunity

8. <u>Digital Detox:</u>

- Regular breaks from social media and digital devices

- Cultivating real-world connections and experiences

9. <u>Nature Connection:</u>

- Spending time in nature to foster a sense of perspective and interconnectedness

- Engaging in environmental stewardship activities

10. <u>Spiritual or Contemplative Practices:</u>

- Engaging with spiritual traditions that emphasise the transcendence of ego

- Contemplative practices like prayer or meditation

Challenges in Personal Transformation:

1. <u>Resistance to Change:</u>

- Overcoming ingrained habits and defence mechanisms

- Navigating discomfort associated with challenging the ego

2. <u>Social Pressures:</u>

- Dealing with societal expectations that may reinforce ego-driven behaviours

- Finding support for personal growth in potentially unsupportive environments

3. <u>Consistency:</u>

   - Maintaining a commitment to practices over time

   - Integrating insights into daily life beyond formal practice sessions

4. <u>Balancing Self-Improvement with Self-Acceptance:</u>

   - Avoiding the trap of perfectionistic striving

   - Cultivating growth while maintaining self-compassion

5. <u>Transferring Insights to Action:</u>

   - Moving beyond intellectual understanding to embodied change

   - Applying personal insights to real-world situations and relationships

Measuring Progress:

1. <u>Self-Assessment Tools:</u>

   - Regular use of validated psychological scales for traits like humility or emotional intelligence

   - Personal inventories and reflection exercises

2. <u>Feedback from Others:</u>

   - Seeking honest input from trusted friends, family, or mentors

   - 360-degree feedback in professional settings

3. <u>Behavioral Indicators:</u>

   - Noticing changes in reactions to challenging situations

   - Observing shifts in interpersonal dynamics

4. <u>Journaling and Self-Reflection:</u>

   - Tracking personal growth and challenges over time

   - Identifying patterns and areas for continued development

As we consider personal transformation the foundation for broader change, key questions emerge: How can we create supportive environments that encourage and sustain personal growth? How can communities, institutions, and technologies facilitate individual transformation? How can personal change efforts be linked to broader societal shifts toward humility, empathy, and wisdom?

3. Interpersonal Dynamics: Fostering Empathy and Connection

Building on personal transformation, this section explores how to cultivate healthier interpersonal dynamics that go beyond ego-driven interactions and foster genuine empathy and connection.

Key Aspects of Healthy Interpersonal Dynamics:

1. <u>Empathetic Communication:</u>

   - Developing active listening skills

   - Practicing perspective-taking and emotional attunement

   - Using "I" statements and non-violent communication techniques

2. <u>Authentic Self-Expression:</u>

   - Cultivating the courage to be vulnerable and genuine

   - Balancing honesty with kindness in communication

   - Expressing needs and boundaries clearly and respectfully

3. <u>Conflict Resolution:</u>

   - Developing skills for constructive disagreement

   - Practicing collaborative problem-solving

   - Cultivating a win-win mentality rather than ego-driven competition

4. <u>Trust-Building:</u>

   - Consistently demonstrating reliability and integrity

   - Being transparent about intentions and limitations

   - Showing vulnerability and admitting mistakes

5. <u>Appreciation and Recognition:</u>

   - Regularly expressing gratitude and acknowledging others' contributions

   - Celebrating diverse strengths and perspectives

   - Fostering a culture of mutual support and encouragement

6. <u>Collaborative Spirit:</u>

   - Cultivating a mindset of interdependence rather than individualism

   - Developing skills for effective teamwork and co-creation

- Balancing individual agency with collective responsibility

7. <u>Cultural Competence:</u>

- Developing awareness and respect for cultural differences

- Practicing inclusivity and creating space for diverse voices

- Addressing unconscious biases and stereotypes

Strategies for Improving Interpersonal Dynamics:

1. <u>Active Listening Workshops:</u>

- Training in techniques like reflective listening and empathetic responding

- Practice sessions for deep listening without interruption or judgment

2. <u>Empathy-Building Exercises:</u>

- Structured activities to practice perspective-taking

- Storytelling circles to share personal experiences and foster understanding

3. <u>Non-Violent Communication Training:</u>

- Learning and practising the NVC model developed by Marshall Rosenberg

- Role-playing exercises to apply NVC in challenging situations

4. <u>Conflict Resolution Skills Development:</u>

- Training in mediation techniques and collaborative problem-solving

- Practice in identifying underlying needs and interests in conflicts

5. <u>Team-Building Activities:</u>

- Structured exercises to build trust and cooperation within groups

- Outdoor or adventure-based programs for shared challenges and bonding

6. <u>Diversity and Inclusion Workshops:</u>

- Educational programs on cultural competence and unconscious bias

- Experiential activities to foster cross-cultural understanding

7. <u>Mentoring and Coaching Programs:</u>

- Pairing individuals for mutual learning and support

- Structured programs for skill-sharing and personal development

8. <u>Appreciation Practices:</u>

- Implementing regular appreciation circles or gratitude-sharing sessions

- Developing systems for peer recognition and celebration of contributions

9. <u>Dialogue Groups:</u>

- Facilitating regular gatherings for deep discussion on meaningful topics

- Creating safe spaces for sharing diverse perspectives and

experiences

10. <u>Technology-Assisted Connection:</u>

- Utilizing digital platforms for meaningful exchange and collaboration

- Developing guidelines for healthy online communication and relationships

Challenges in Improving Interpersonal Dynamics:

1. <u>Overcoming Ingrained Patterns:</u>

- Addressing deeply held beliefs and habitual reactions

- Navigating resistance to change in interpersonal styles

2. <u>Power Dynamics:</u>

- Addressing imbalances of power and privilege in relationships

- Cultivating authentic connections across hierarchical structures

3. <u>Cultural Differences:</u>

- Navigating diverse communication styles and cultural norms

- Addressing language barriers and differing worldviews

4. <u>Digital Communication:</u>

- Maintaining empathy and connection in online interactions

- Balancing digital convenience with the need for in-person connection

5. <u>Maintaining Boundaries:</u>

- Balancing openness and vulnerability with healthy personal boundaries

- Addressing issues of co-dependency or over-reliance

6. <u>Scaling Interpersonal Skills:</u>

- Translating one-on-one skills to group and organisational dynamics

- Maintaining authentic connection in larger social contexts

Measuring Progress in Interpersonal Dynamics:

1. <u>Relationship Satisfaction Surveys:</u>

- Regular assessments of relationship quality in various contexts

- Feedback mechanisms for ongoing improvement

2. <u>Conflict Resolution Metrics:</u>

- Tracking the frequency and nature of conflicts

- Assessing the effectiveness of resolution processes

3. <u>Team Performance Indicators:</u>

- Measuring collaboration effectiveness and team cohesion

- Assessing the impact of improved dynamics on productivity and innovation

4. <u>Empathy and Emotional Intelligence Assessments:</u>

- Using validated tools to measure growth in these areas

- Peer and self-assessments of interpersonal skills

5. <u>Cultural Competence Evaluations:</u>

- Assessing growth in cross-cultural understanding and effectiveness

- Measuring inclusivity and diversity in social networks and collaborations

As we consider cultivating healthier interpersonal dynamics, key questions emerge: How can we create societal structures that encourage and reward empathetic and collaborative behaviours? What role can education systems play in developing these crucial interpersonal skills from an early age? How might improved interpersonal dynamics at a micro level contribute to addressing more significant societal challenges and conflicts?

4. Organizational Change: Reimagining Leadership and Structures

This section builds on personal and interpersonal transformations to explore how organisations can evolve to foster environments that discourage ego-driven behaviours and promote collective wisdom and well-being.

Key Aspects of Organizational Transformation:

1. <u>Servant Leadership:</u>

- Promoting leadership models that prioritise serving others over self-interest

- Developing leaders who empower and support their teams

- Cultivating a culture of humility and continuous learning at all levels

2. <u>Flatter Hierarchies:</u>

   - Reducing excessive layers of management

   - Implementing more democratic decision-making processes

   - Fostering a culture of open communication across all levels

3. <u>Purpose-Driven Organizations:</u>

   - Clearly articulating and embodying organisational values and purpose

   - Aligning business practices with broader societal and environmental benefits

   - Measuring success beyond financial metrics

4. <u>Collaborative Structures:</u>

   - Implementing team-based and project-based work structures

   - Encouraging cross-functional collaboration and knowledge sharing

   - Utilizing collective intelligence through participatory processes

5. <u>Transparency and Accountability:</u>

   - Increasing transparency in decision-making and financial matters

   - Implementing fair and consistent accountability measures

   - Encouraging open feedback and constructive criticism

6. <u>Learning Organizations:</u>

- Fostering a culture of continuous learning and adaptation

- Encouraging experimentation and viewing failures as learning opportunities

- Implementing systems for knowledge sharing and collective growth

7. <u>Diversity and Inclusion:</u>

- Actively promoting diversity at all levels of the organisation

- Creating inclusive environments that value diverse perspectives

- Addressing systemic biases in hiring, promotion, and daily operations

8. <u>Well-being Focus:</u>

- Prioritizing employee well-being and work-life balance

- Implementing programs for mental health support and stress reduction

- Creating physical environments that promote health and collaboration

Strategies for Organizational Transformation:

1. <u>Leadership Development Programs:</u>

- Training focused on servant leadership principles

- Emotional intelligence and empathy development for leaders

- Mentoring and coaching programs for emerging leaders

2. <u>Organizational Structure Redesign:</u>

- Consultative processes to reimagine hierarchies and reporting structures

- Piloting new organisational models (e.g., holacracy, sociocracy)

- Implementing agile methodologies beyond IT departments

3. <u>Purpose and Values Alignment:</u>

- Collaborative processes to define or refine organisational purpose

- Regular assessments of alignment between stated values and actual practices

- Integrating purpose into all aspects of operations and decision-making

4. <u>Collaborative Technologies:</u>

- Implementing digital platforms for enhanced collaboration and communication

- Utilizing AI and data analytics for more informed and participatory decision-making

- Developing guidelines for ethical use of technology in the workplace

5. <u>Transparency Initiatives:</u>

- Open-book management practices

- Regular town halls and open forums for organisational updates and feedback

- Implementing blockchain or other technologies for

enhanced transparency

6. <u>Learning and Development Programs:</u>

- Allocating resources for ongoing employee education and skill development

- Creating internal knowledge-sharing platforms and communities of practice

- Partnerships with educational institutions for lifelong learning opportunities

7. <u>Diversity and Inclusion Strategies:</u>

- Comprehensive D&I training programs

- Implementing blind hiring practices and diverse interview panels

- Creating employee resource groups and mentoring programs for underrepresented groups

8. <u>Well-being and Mental Health Initiatives:</u>

- Flexible work arrangements and policies that support work-life balance

- On-site wellness programs and mental health resources

- Redesigning physical spaces to promote well-being and collaboration

9. <u>Stakeholder Engagement:</u>

- Expanding the concept of stakeholders beyond shareholders

- Regular dialogue with community members, customers, and other stakeholders

- Implementing stakeholder-inclusive decision-making processes

10. <u>Measurement and Feedback Systems:</u>

- Developing holistic metrics that go beyond financial performance

- Implementing regular 360-degree feedback processes

- Utilizing AI and data analytics for real-time performance and well-being monitoring

Challenges in Organizational Transformation:

1. <u>Resistance to Change:</u>

- Overcoming entrenched power structures and vested interests

- Addressing fear and uncertainty among employees

2. <u>Short-Term Pressures:</u>

- Balancing long-term transformation with short-term performance demands

- Navigating shareholder expectations in publicly traded companies

3. <u>Scale and Complexity:</u>

- Implementing changes consistently across large or geographically dispersed organisations

- Managing the complexity of interrelated systems in organisational change

4. <u>Cultural Shift:</u>

- Changing deeply ingrained organisational cultures and mindsets

- Aligning subcultures within different departments or regions

5. <u>Skill Gaps:</u>

- Developing new competencies required for transformed organisational structures

- Retraining or transitioning employees whose roles become obsolete

6. <u>Technological Adaptation:</u>

- Ensuring equitable access and proficiency in new collaborative technologies

- Addressing concerns about privacy and surveillance in digital work environments

7. <u>Legal and Regulatory Constraints:</u>

- Navigating legal structures that may not easily accommodate new organisational models

- Ensuring compliance while implementing innovative practices

8. <u>Measuring Impact:</u>

- Developing new metrics to assess the success of organisational transformations

- Balancing quantitative and qualitative measures of progress

9. <u>Maintaining Momentum:</u>

- Sustaining enthusiasm and commitment to change over the long term

- Navigating setbacks and adjusting strategies without losing sight of the overall vision

Measuring Progress in Organizational Transformation:

1. Employee Engagement Surveys:

- Regular assessments of job satisfaction, sense of purpose, and alignment with organisational values

- Tracking changes in employee perceptions over time

2. Leadership Effectiveness Metrics:

- 360-degree feedback on leadership behaviours

- Assessing the adoption and effectiveness of servant leadership practices

3. Diversity and Inclusion Indicators:

- Tracking representation at all levels of the organisation

- Measuring inclusion through employee experience surveys and retention rates

4. Innovation and Adaptability Measures:

- Assessing the organisation's ability to respond to change and generate new ideas

- Tracking the implementation and impact of employee-driven innovations

5. Stakeholder Satisfaction:

- Regular surveys of customers, community members, and

other stakeholders

- Measuring the organisation's impact on broader societal and environmental issues

6. <u>Financial and Non-Financial Performance:</u>

- Balanced scorecards that include social and environmental metrics alongside financial ones

- Long-term value creation measures that go beyond quarterly earnings

7. <u>Collaboration and Knowledge Sharing Metrics:</u>

- Assessing the effectiveness of cross-functional teams and projects

- Measuring the use and impact of knowledge-sharing platforms

8. <u>Well-being and Health Indicators:</u>

- Tracking employee health and well-being through various measures

- Assessing the impact of well-being initiatives on productivity and retention

As we consider organisational transformation a key element in addressing ego and arrogance in society, several important questions arise: How can organisations balance the need for structure and efficiency with more egalitarian and collaborative models? What role can business play in promoting broader societal shifts towards humility and collective well-being? And how might transformed organisations contribute to solving complex global challenges?

5. Societal Shifts: Addressing Systemic Issues and Cultural Narratives

While individual, interpersonal, and organisational changes are crucial, lasting transformation requires addressing broader societal structures and cultural narratives. This section explores how we can foster societal shifts discouraging ego-driven behaviours and promoting collective flourishing.

Key Aspects of Societal Transformation:

1. <u>Redefining Success:</u>

   - Shifting cultural narratives away from materialism and status-seeking

   - Promoting definitions of success that include well-being, relationships, and contribution to society

   - Celebrating diverse forms of achievement beyond wealth and fame

2. <u>Education Reform:</u>

   - Redesigning educational systems to foster creativity, critical thinking, and emotional intelligence

   - Incorporating ethics, mindfulness, and systems thinking into curricula at all levels

   - Promoting lifelong learning and adaptability

3. <u>Economic Restructuring:</u>

   - Exploring alternative economic models that prioritise well-being and sustainability

   - Implementing policies to address wealth inequality and ensure basic needs are met

- Encouraging business models that internalize social and environmental costs

4. <u>Media and Information Ecosystems:</u>

- Promoting media literacy and critical thinking skills

- Supporting independent journalism and diverse voices in media

- Addressing the challenges of misinformation and echo chambers in digital spaces

5. <u>Political Systems:</u>

- Implementing reforms to reduce the influence of money in politics

- Exploring more participatory forms of democracy

- Promoting long-term thinking in policy-making

6. <u>Social Safety Nets:</u>

- Strengthening systems that provide essential security and dignity for all members of society

- Exploring universal basic income or similar programs

- Ensuring access to quality healthcare, education, and housing

7. <u>Environmental Stewardship:</u>

- Embedding ecological consciousness into all aspects of society

- Implementing policies and practices for sustainable resource use

- Fostering a sense of connection and responsibility to the natural world

8. <u>Cultural Diversity and Inclusion:</u>

- Celebrating and preserving cultural diversity

- Addressing systemic racism and other forms of discrimination

- Promoting intercultural dialogue and understanding

9. <u>Technology Ethics:</u>

- Developing ethical frameworks for emerging technologies

- Ensuring that technological development serves human and ecological well-being

- Addressing issues of privacy, autonomy, and equity in the digital age

Strategies for Societal Transformation:

1. <u>Policy and Legislation:</u>

- Implementing laws and policies that incentivise socially and environmentally responsible behaviours

- Creating regulatory frameworks that hold institutions accountable for their societal impact

2. <u>Public Awareness Campaigns:</u>

- Large-scale educational initiatives on key societal issues

- Using various media channels to promote new cultural narratives

3. <u>Community-Based Initiatives:</u>

- Supporting grassroots movements and local community projects

- Fostering neighbourhood-level resilience and mutual aid networks

4. <u>Cross-Sector Collaborations:</u>

- Easing partnerships between government, business, academia, and civil society

- Creating platforms for collective problem-solving on complex societal issues

5. <u>Arts and Culture:</u>

- Supporting artists and cultural creators who promote alternative visions of society

- Utilizing the power of storytelling and cultural expression to shift narratives

6. <u>Technology for Social Good:</u>

- Developing and promoting technologies that address societal challenges

- Creating open-source platforms for collective intelligence and problem-solving

7. <u>Educational Innovations:</u>

- Supporting alternative educational models and experiments

- Integrating real-world problem-solving into educational curricula

8. <u>Economic Experiments:</u>

- Piloting new economic models at local or regional levels

- Supporting the development of alternative currencies and exchange systems

9. <u>Mindfulness and Contemplative Practices:</u>

- Promoting widespread adoption of practices that foster self-awareness and compassion

- Integrating contemplative practices into various societal institutions

10. <u>Intergenerational Dialogue:</u>

- Creating platforms for exchange between different age groups

- Fostering long-term thinking by connecting past, present, and future perspectives

Challenges in Societal Transformation:

1. <u>Inertia and Resistance:</u>

- Overcoming deeply entrenched systems and power structures

- Addressing fear of change and loss of privilege

2. <u>Complexity and Interconnectedness:</u>

- Navigating the intricate web of societal systems and their interdependencies

- Avoiding unintended consequences of well-intentioned changes

3. <u>Short-Term Thinking:</u>

- Overcoming political and economic systems that prioritise short-term gains

- Building public support for long-term investments and policies

4. <u>Global Coordination:</u>

- Addressing global challenges that require coordinated action across nations

- Navigating cultural differences and competing national interests

5. <u>Technological Disruption:</u>

- Managing the societal impacts of rapid technological change

- Ensuring that technological progress aligns with human values and well-being

6. <u>Information Overload and Misinformation:</u>

- Helping individuals navigate complex information landscapes

- Combating deliberate misinformation and conspiracy theories

7. <u>Balancing Unity and Diversity:</u>

- Fostering a sense of shared purpose while respecting cultural differences

- Addressing polarisation and finding common ground across divides

Measuring Progress in Societal Transformation:

1. <u>Well-being Indices:</u>

   - Utilizing comprehensive measures of societal health beyond GDP

   - Tracking indicators of social cohesion, environmental sustainability, and individual flourishing

2. <u>Equality and Inclusion Metrics:</u>

   - Measuring progress in reducing various forms of inequality

   - Assessing the inclusivity of societal institutions and cultural narratives

3. <u>Environmental Indicators:</u>

   - Tracking ecological footprints and progress towards sustainability goals

   - Measuring biodiversity, air and water quality, and other environmental health indicators

4. <u>Civic Engagement Measures:</u>

   - Assessing levels of political participation and community involvement

   - Measuring trust in institutions and social cohesion

5. <u>Education and Skill Development:</u>

   - Tracking not just academic achievements but also creativity, emotional intelligence, and adaptability

   - Measuring lifelong learning and skill development across the population

6. <u>Media and Information Quality:</u>

- Assessing the diversity and reliability of information ecosystems

- Measuring levels of media literacy and critical thinking skills in the population

7. <u>Technological Ethics:</u>

- Developing metrics to assess the ethical implications of technological developments

- Measuring public understanding and engagement with tech ethics issues

As we consider these broader societal shifts, key questions emerge: How can we build momentum for large-scale change while respecting democratic processes and individual freedoms? What role can various sectors of society (government, business, education, civil society) play in fostering these transformations? And how do we balance the need for global coordination with respect for local and cultural diversity in addressing shared challenges?

6. Global Perspectives: Navigating International Challenges

Many challenges in our interconnected world transcend national boundaries and require global cooperation. This section explores how we can address international issues while fostering a sense of shared humanity and collective responsibility.

Key Aspects of Global Cooperation:

1. <u>Shared Global Ethics:</u>

- Developing and promoting universal ethical principles that transcend cultural differences

- Fostering a sense of global citizenship and shared responsibility

2. <u>International Governance:</u>

- Strengthening and reforming international institutions

- Developing more effective mechanisms for global decision-making and conflict resolution

3. <u>Global Economic Justice:</u>

- Addressing inequalities between nations and regions

- Developing fair trade practices and sustainable development initiatives

4. <u>Climate Change and Environmental Protection:</u>

- Coordinating global efforts to address climate change and protect biodiversity

- Developing and implementing international environmental agreements

5. <u>Peace and Conflict Resolution:</u>

- Strengthening international peacekeeping and conflict prevention mechanisms

- Promoting dialogue and understanding between nations and cultures

6. <u>Global Health:</u>

- Coordinating responses to global health challenges and pandemics

- Ensuring equitable access to healthcare and medical innovations worldwide

7. <u>Technology Governance:</u>

- Developing international frameworks for emerging technologies like AI and genetic engineering

- Addressing global cybersecurity challenges

8. <u>Cultural Exchange and Understanding:</u>

- Promoting cross-cultural dialogue and appreciation of diversity

- Preserving and celebrating cultural heritage in a globalised world

Strategies for Global Cooperation:

1. <u>Multilateral Agreements and Institutions:</u>

- Strengthening existing international organisations like the UN

- Developing new multilateral frameworks for emerging global challenges

2. <u>Global Civil Society Networks:</u>

- Supporting international NGOs and civil society coalitions

- Facilitating global citizen movements and grassroots international cooperation

3. <u>International Scientific Collaboration:</u>

- Fostering global research networks to address shared challenges

- Ensuring open access to scientific knowledge and data

4. <u>Global Education Initiatives:</u>

- Promoting international education exchanges and collaborations

- Developing global citizenship education programs

5. <u>Digital Platforms for Global Dialogue:</u>

- Creating online spaces for cross-cultural exchange and collaborative problem-solving

- Utilizing technology to facilitate global participatory decision-making

6. <u>International Business Responsibility:</u>

- Developing and enforcing global standards for corporate social and environmental responsibility

- Encouraging businesses to address global challenges through their operations and innovations

7. <u>Arts and Cultural Diplomacy:</u>

- Using arts and cultural exchange to foster international understanding

- Preserving and sharing diverse cultural heritage globally

8. <u>Global Media and Communication:</u>

- Supporting international journalism and diverse global voices

- Addressing language barriers and promoting multilingual communication

9. <u>Interfaith and Intercultural Dialogue:</u>

- Facilitating dialogues between different religious and cultural traditions

- Finding common ground and shared values across diverse worldviews

Challenges in Global Cooperation:

1. <u>National Sovereignty:</u>

   - Balancing global governance with respect for national self-determination

   - Addressing concerns about loss of local control and identity

2. <u>Power Imbalances:</u>

   - Navigating disparities in economic and political power between nations

   - Ensuring fair representation in global decision-making processes

3. <u>Cultural Differences:</u>

   - Respecting diverse cultural values while finding common ethical ground

   - Overcoming language barriers and misunderstandings

4. <u>Short-Term National Interests:</u>

   - Aligning short-term national priorities with long-term global needs

   - Building political will for international cooperation

5. <u>Complexity of Global Systems:</u>

   - Managing the intricate interdependencies of global economic, environmental, and social systems

- Avoiding unintended consequences in global interventions

6. <u>Information Integrity:</u>

- Combating misinformation and propaganda at a global scale

- Ensuring accurate and diverse sources of global information

7. <u>Technological Divides:</u>

- Addressing disparities in access to and benefits from global technologies

- Ensuring that technological advancements serve global well-being equitably

Measuring Progress in Global Cooperation:

1. <u>Sustainable Development Goals:</u>

- Tracking progress on the UN's SDGs and other global benchmarks

- Developing more nuanced and culturally sensitive global indicators

2. <u>Global Peace and Conflict Indices:</u>

- Measuring levels of international conflict and cooperation

- Assessing the effectiveness of global peacekeeping and conflict resolution efforts

3. <u>Global Economic Indicators:</u>

- Tracking global inequality and progress towards more equitable economic systems

- Measuring the growth of sustainable and ethical global business practices

4. <u>Environmental and Climate Metrics:</u>

- Monitoring global progress on climate change mitigation and adaptation

- Tracking global biodiversity and ecosystem health

5. <u>Global Health Statistics:</u>

- Measuring progress on global health challenges and equity in healthcare access

- Assessing the global ability to respond to health crises

6. <u>International Collaboration Indices:</u>

- Tracking levels of scientific, cultural, and educational international collaborations

- Measuring global civil society networks and citizen engagement in global issues

7. <u>Technological Ethics:</u>

- Ensuring Human Values Guide Our Technological Future

As technology advances at an unprecedented pace, we must develop ethical frameworks to guide its development and use. This section explores how we can ensure that our technological future aligns with human values and contributes to collective well-being.

Key Aspects of Technological Ethics:

1. <u>Human-Centred Design:</u>

- Prioritizing human needs and well-being in technological

development

- Ensuring technology enhances rather than replaces human capabilities

2. <u>Privacy and Data Protection:</u>

- Developing robust frameworks for data privacy and security

- Empowering individuals with control over their data

3. <u>Algorithmic Fairness and Transparency:</u>

- Addressing biases in AI and machine learning systems

- Ensuring transparency and accountability in algorithmic decision-making

4. <u>Digital Inclusion:</u>

- Bridging the digital divide and ensuring fair access to technology

- Developing technologies that are accessible to diverse populations

5. <u>Environmental Sustainability:</u>

- Minimizing the environmental impact of technology

- Using technology to address environmental challenges

6. <u>Ethical AI Development:</u>

- Setting up principles for the responsible development of artificial intelligence

- Addressing existential risks associated with advanced AI

7. <u>Biotechnology and Human Enhancement:</u>

   - Navigating ethical issues in genetic engineering and human augmentation

   - Balancing potential benefits with risks and ethical concerns

8. <u>Digital Well-being:</u>

   - Addressing issues of technology addiction and mental health

   - Designing technologies that promote healthy use patterns

Strategies for Implementing Technological Ethics:

1. <u>Ethical Guidelines and Frameworks:</u>

   - Developing comprehensive ethical guidelines for technology development and use

   - Implementing ethics review boards for technological research and development

2. <u>Interdisciplinary Collaboration:</u>

   - Fostering collaboration between technologists, ethicists, social scientists, and policymakers

   - Integrating diverse perspectives in technological decision-making

3. <u>Ethics Education for Technologists:</u>

   - Incorporating ethics courses into STEM education

   - Providing ongoing ethics training for technology professionals

4. <u>Public Engagement and Dialogue:</u>

   - Facilitating public discussions on the ethical implications of emerging technologies

   - Involving diverse stakeholders in shaping technological policies

5. <u>Regulatory Frameworks:</u>

   - Developing adaptive regulations that can keep pace with technological change

   - Implementing international agreements on technological ethics

6. <u>Ethical Certification Programs:</u>

   - Creating certification systems for ethically developed technologies

   - Promoting transparency in the ethical practices of tech companies

7. <u>Responsible Innovation Practices:</u>

   - Implementing methodologies like Value Sensitive Design in technology development

   - Encouraging long-term thinking and consideration of societal impacts in innovation

Challenges in Technological Ethics:

1. <u>Rapid Pace of Change:</u>

   - Keeping ethical frameworks and regulations up-to-date with fast-moving technological advancements

   - Predicting and addressing ethical issues of future

technologies

2. <u>Global Coordination:</u>

   - Developing international consensus on technological ethics

   - Addressing cultural differences in ethical perspectives on technology

3. <u>Balancing Innovation and Caution:</u>

   - Encouraging technological progress while mitigating risks

   - Navigating tensions between precautionary principles and pro-actionary imperatives

4. <u>Complexity of Ethical Issues:</u>

   - Addressing multifaceted ethical dilemmas without clear solutions

   - Dealing with unintended consequences of technological implementations

5. <u>Power Dynamics:</u>

   - Addressing the concentration of power in large tech companies

   - Ensuring democratic control over the direction of technological development

Measuring Progress in Technological Ethics:

1. <u>Ethical Impact Assessments:</u>

   - Developing and implementing comprehensive frameworks for assessing the ethical impact of technologies

- Regular auditing of AI systems for fairness and bias

2. <u>Public Trust Indicators:</u>

- Measuring public trust and confidence in technological systems and institutions

- Assessing public understanding of technological ethical issues

3. <u>Digital Well-being Metrics:</u>

- Tracking indicators of healthy technology use and digital well-being

- Measuring the impact of technologies on mental health and social cohesion

4. <u>Sustainability Metrics:</u>

- Assessing the environmental impact of technological development and use

- Measuring the contribution of technology to environmental solutions

5. <u>Inclusivity and Accessibility Measures:</u>

- Tracking progress in bridging the digital divide

- Measuring the accessibility of technologies for diverse populations

As we navigate the complex landscape of technological ethics, key questions emerge: How can we create systems of governance that can effectively guide technological development in rapidly changing environments? How do we balance the potential benefits of technological advancement with ethical concerns and possible risks? And how can we ensure that our technological future enhances human flourishing and aligns with our deepest values?

8. Environmental Stewardship: Cultivating a Sustainable Relationship with Our Planet

As we face unprecedented environmental challenges, fostering a culture of environmental stewardship is crucial for our collective future. This section explores how we can cultivate a more sustainable and harmonious relationship with the natural world.

Key Aspects of Environmental Stewardship:

1. <u>Ecological Consciousness:</u>

   - Fostering a deep understanding of ecological systems and humanity's place within them

   - Developing an ethic of care and responsibility towards the natural world

2. <u>Sustainable Resource Management:</u>

   - Implementing practices for the sustainable use of natural resources

   - Transitioning to circular economy models that minimise waste and maximise efficiency

3. <u>Climate Change Mitigation and Adaptation:</u>

   - Reducing greenhouse gas emissions across all sectors of society

   - Developing resilience strategies for adapting to changing climate conditions

4. <u>Biodiversity Conservation:</u>

- Protecting and restoring habitats to preserve biodiversity

- Addressing human activities that threaten species and ecosystems

5. <u>Sustainable Agriculture and Food Systems:</u>

- Promoting regenerative agricultural practices

- Developing food systems that are environmentally sustainable and socially just

6. <u>Clean Energy Transition:</u>

- Accelerating the shift to renewable energy sources

- Improving energy efficiency across all sectors

7. <u>Urban Sustainability:</u>

- Designing cities that are environmentally friendly and liveable

- Integrating nature into urban environments

8. <u>Environmental Justice:</u>

- Addressing disparities in environmental impacts on different communities

- Ensuring equitable access to natural resources and healthy environments

Strategies for Promoting Environmental Stewardship:

1. <u>Education and Awareness:</u>

- Integrating environmental education into school curricula at all levels

- Conducting public awareness campaigns on environmental issues

2. <u>Policy and Legislation:</u>

- Implementing strong environmental protection laws and regulations

- Using economic incentives to promote sustainable practices

3. <u>Technological Innovation:</u>

- Developing and deploying clean technologies

- Using AI and data analytics for environmental monitoring and management

4. <u>Community Engagement:</u>

- Supporting local environmental initiatives and citizen science projects

- Fostering a connection with nature through outdoor education and experiences

5. <u>Sustainable Business Practices:</u>

- Promoting corporate environmental responsibility

- Developing markets for sustainable products and services

6. <u>International Cooperation:</u>

- Strengthening global environmental agreements and institutions

- Easing knowledge sharing and technology transfer for environmental solutions

7. <u>Indigenous Wisdom Integration:</u>

- Learning from and supporting Indigenous environmental stewardship practices

- Protecting Indigenous land rights and traditional ecological knowledge

8. <u>Regenerative Design:</u>

- Applying principles of regenerative design in architecture, urban planning, and product design

- Developing systems that restore and enhance ecosystem health

Challenges in Environmental Stewardship:

1. <u>Economic Pressures:</u>

- Balancing short-term economic interests with long-term environmental sustainability

- Transitioning to sustainable economic models without causing social disruption

2. <u>Behavioural Change:</u>

- Overcoming ingrained habits and lifestyles that are environmentally unsustainable

- Motivating individual and collective action on environmental issues

3. <u>Political Will:</u>

- Building political support for strong environmental policies

- Addressing the influence of vested interests opposed to

environmental action

4. <u>Global Coordination:</u>

   - Coordinating effective global responses to transnational environmental challenges

   - Ensuring equitable distribution of responsibilities and resources in environmental efforts

5. <u>Technological Limitations:</u>

   - Developing and scaling up technologies needed for sustainability transitions

   - Addressing potential adverse environmental impacts of modern technologies

Measuring Progress in Environmental Stewardship:

1. <u>Ecological Footprint Assessments:</u>

   - Measuring human demand on natural resources relative to Earth's ecological capacity

   - Tracking progress in reducing individual and collective ecological footprints

2. <u>Biodiversity Indicators:</u>

   - Monitoring species populations and ecosystem health

   - Assessing the effectiveness of conservation efforts

3. <u>Climate Metrics:</u>

   - Tracking greenhouse gas emissions and progress towards emissions reduction targets

   - Measuring adaptive capacity to climate change impacts

4. <u>Resource Use Efficiency:</u>

   - Assessing improvements in energy, water, and material use efficiency

   - Measuring progress towards circular economy models

5. <u>Environmental Quality Indices:</u>

   - Monitoring air, water, and soil quality

   - Tracking the health of various ecosystems

6. <u>Sustainability in Business:</u>

   - Measuring corporate adoption of sustainable practices

   - Assessing the growth of markets for sustainable products and services

7. <u>Public Engagement Metrics:</u>

   - Measuring public knowledge and attitudes towards environmental issues

   - Tracking participation in environmental initiatives and behaviours

As we consider ecological stewardship, key questions arise: How can we create economic systems that align with ecological realities? What cultural shifts are needed to foster a widespread ethic of environmental care? And how can we ensure that efforts towards sustainability also promote social justice and human well-being?

9. Education and Lifelong Learning: Preparing for an Uncertain Future

Education and continuous learning are crucial for navigating challenges and seizing opportunities in a rapidly changing world. This section explores how we can reimagine education to foster adaptability, critical thinking, and a lifelong love of learning.

Key Aspects of Future-Oriented Education:

1. Adaptive Skills Development:

- Focusing on transferable skills like critical thinking, creativity, and emotional intelligence

- Preparing learners for jobs that may not yet exist

2. Interdisciplinary Learning:

- Breaking down silos between academic disciplines

- Fostering systems thinking and holistic problem-solving abilities

3. Digital Literacy:

- Developing competencies for navigating and critically engaging with digital environments

- Teaching responsible and ethical use of technology

4. Global Citizenship Education:

- Cultivating an understanding of global issues and interconnectedness

- Fostering cross-cultural competence and empathy

5. Environmental and Sustainability Education:

- Integrating ecological literacy across curricula

- Developing skills for sustainable living and problem-solving

6. <u>Personalized Learning:</u>

- Utilizing technology to tailor education to individual needs and learning styles

- Empowering learners to take ownership of their educational journeys

7. <u>Experiential and Project-Based Learning:</u>

- Emphasizing hands-on, real-world application of knowledge

- Fostering collaboration and practical problem-solving skills

8. <u>Lifelong Learning Infrastructure:</u>

- Creating systems and cultures that support continuous learning throughout life

- Developing flexible credentialing and skill recognition systems

Strategies for Transforming Education:

1. <u>Curriculum Redesign:</u>

- Updating curricula to reflect 21st-century skills and knowledge needs

- Incorporating flexibility to adapt to emerging fields and challenges

2. <u>Teacher Training and Support:</u>

- Equipping educators with skills for facilitating future-oriented learning

- Providing ongoing professional development and resources

3. <u>Technology Integration:</u>

- Leveraging AI, VR, and other technologies to enhance learning experiences

- Ensuring equitable access to educational technologies

4. <u>Community Partnerships:</u>

- Collaborating with businesses, non-profits, and community organisations for real-world learning opportunities

- Integrating service learning into educational programs

5. <u>Assessment Reform:</u>

- Developing new methods for evaluating complex skills and competencies

- Moving beyond standardised testing to more holistic assessment approaches

6. <u>Open Educational Resources:</u>

- Promoting the creation and use of freely accessible educational materials

- Leveraging technology for global knowledge sharing

7. <u>Intergenerational Learning Programs:</u>

- Creating opportunities for knowledge exchange between different age groups

- Valuing and integrating diverse life experiences in learning contexts

8. <u>Mindfulness and Well-being Education:</u>

   - Incorporating practices for mental health and emotional well-being into curricula

   - Teaching stress management and resilience skills

Challenges in Educational Transformation:

1. <u>Systemic Inertia:</u>

   - Overcoming resistance to change in established educational institutions

   - Addressing entrenched interests and traditional metrics of success

2. <u>Equity and Access:</u>

   - Ensuring that educational innovations benefit all learners, not just the privileged

   - Bridging digital divides and other barriers to access

3. <u>Balancing Tradition and Innovation:</u>

   - Preserving valuable aspects of traditional education while embracing necessary changes

   - Navigating diverse cultural perspectives on the purpose and methods of education

4. <u>Rapid Pace of Change:</u>

   - Keeping educational content and methods relevant in a fast-changing world

   - Preparing learners for an uncertain future job market

5. <u>Funding and Resources:</u>

- Securing adequate funding for educational transformation

- Addressing disparities in resources between different schools and regions

Measuring Progress in Education:

1. <u>Adaptive Skill Assessments:</u>

- Developing and implementing measures for critical thinking, creativity, and other key adaptive skills

- Tracking long-term outcomes of educational approaches

2. <u>Learner Engagement Metrics:</u>

- Measuring student motivation, curiosity, and love of learning

- Assessing the relevance and effectiveness of learning experiences

3. <u>Global Competence Indicators:</u>

- Evaluating cross-cultural understanding and global awareness

- Measuring participation in international and cross-cultural learning experiences

4. <u>Lifelong Learning Participation:</u>

- Tracking engagement in continuing education and skill development throughout life

- Assessing the accessibility and effectiveness of lifelong learning opportunities

5. <u>Well-being and Resilience Measures:</u>

- Evaluating the impact of education on mental health and emotional well-being

- Assessing learners' ability to navigate challenges and uncertainty

As we reimagine education for the future, key questions emerge: How can we create educational systems that are both globally relevant and locally responsive? What is the right balance between specialised knowledge and generalist skills in preparing for an uncertain future? How can education foster individual success, collective wisdom, and societal progress?

10. Spiritual and Philosophical Integration: Finding Meaning and Purpose in a Complex World

Integrating spiritual and philosophical perspectives can provide guidance, meaning, and a sense of purpose as we navigate the complexities of the modern world. This section explores how to draw upon diverse wisdom traditions to address contemporary challenges.

Key Aspects of Spiritual and Philosophical Integration:

1. <u>Holistic Worldviews:</u>

- Cultivating perspectives that recognise the interconnectedness of all things

- Integrating scientific understanding with spiritual and philosophical insights

2. <u>Ethical Frameworks:</u>

- Drawing upon diverse philosophical and spiritual traditions to inform ethical decision-making

- Developing universal ethical principles that can guide

global cooperation

3. <u>Meaning and Purpose:</u>

   - Exploring existential questions and the search for meaning in a scientific age

   - Fostering a sense of purpose that transcends individual ego

4. <u>Contemplative Practices:</u>

   - Integrating mindfulness, meditation, and other contemplative practices into daily life

   - Using these practices to enhance self-awareness and compassion

5. <u>Interfaith and Intercultural Dialogue:</u>

   - Promoting understanding and cooperation between different faiths and cultural traditions

   - Finding common ground while respecting diversity

6. <u>Science-Spirituality Dialogue:</u>

   - Exploring the relationships between scientific and spiritual ways of knowing

   - Using both to inform our understanding of reality and human experience

7. <u>Eco-Spirituality:</u>

   - Fostering spiritual connections with the natural world

   - Integrating environmental stewardship with spiritual practice

8. <u>Social Engagement:</u>

- Applying spiritual and philosophical insights to address social and global challenges

- Balancing inner development with outer action

Strategies for Spiritual and Philosophical Integration:

1. <u>Interfaith Initiatives:</u>

- Supporting programs that bring together diverse spiritual and philosophical traditions

- Creating spaces for dialogue and collaborative action

2. <u>Contemplative Education:</u>

- Incorporating mindfulness and other contemplative practices into educational settings

- Teaching philosophical inquiry and existential reflection skills

3. <u>Spiritual Ecology Movements:</u>

- Supporting initiatives that combine environmental action with spiritual practice

- Promoting worldviews that recognise the sacredness of nature

4. <u>Science-Religion Dialogues:</u>

- Facilitating conversations between scientific and religious leaders

- Exploring areas of convergence and complementarity

5. <u>Ethical Leadership Programs:</u>

- Developing leadership training that integrates spiritual

and philosophical wisdom

- Promoting value-based decision-making in various sectors

6. <u>Community Philosophy Practices:</u>

- Supporting community-based philosophical inquiry and dialogue

- Creating spaces for collective exploration of life's big questions

7. <u>Holistic Health Approaches:</u>

- Integrating spiritual and philosophical perspectives into healthcare

- Promoting well-being practices that address body, mind, and spirit

8. <u>Arts and Culture Initiatives:</u>

- Supporting artistic expressions that explore spiritual and philosophical themes

- Using cultural practices to bridge different worldviews

Challenges in Spiritual and Philosophical Integration:

1. <u>Secularization and Skepticism:</u>

- Addressing scepticism towards spiritual and religious perspectives in secular societies

- Finding ways to articulate spiritual insights in non-dogmatic language

2. <u>Fundamentalism and Intolerance:</u>

- Countering rigid and intolerant interpretations of spiritual traditions

- Promoting openness and dialogue while respecting deeply held beliefs

3. <u>Materialism and Consumerism:</u>

- Addressing cultural values that prioritise material success over spiritual growth

- Fostering an appreciation for non-material sources of fulfilment

4. <u>Complexity and Uncertainty:</u>

- Navigating the complexities of modern life while maintaining spiritual groundedness

- Developing comfort with uncertainty and ambiguity

5. <u>Integration with Secular Institutions:</u>

- Finding appropriate ways to incorporate spiritual perspectives in secular contexts

- Addressing concerns about separation of church and state

Measuring Progress in Spiritual and Philosophical Integration:

1. <u>Well-being and Life Satisfaction Metrics:</u>

- Assessing the impact of spiritual and philosophical practices on overall well-being

- Measuring sense of meaning and purpose in life

2. <u>Social Cohesion Indicators:</u>

- Evaluating the impact of interfaith and intercultural

initiatives on social harmony

- Measuring levels of empathy and compassion in society

3. <u>Ethical Decision-Making Assessments:</u>

- Evaluating the application of ethical frameworks in various sectors

- Measuring public trust in institutions and leaders

4. <u>Environmental Stewardship Metrics:</u>

- Assessing the impact of eco-spiritual perspectives on environmental behaviours

- Measuring a sense of connection with nature

5. <u>Contemplative Practice Engagement:</u>

- Tracking participation in mindfulness and other contemplative practices

- Assessing the integration of these practices in various sectors of society

As we consider integrating spiritual and philosophical perspectives, key questions arise: How can we foster a global ethos that draws upon diverse wisdom traditions while respecting secular viewpoints? What role can spiritual and philosophical insights play in addressing global challenges like climate change and social injustice? How can we cultivate depth and meaning in a fast-paced, technologically driven world?

11. Conclusion: Embracing Humility and Collective Wisdom

As we conclude our exploration of the way forward, it becomes clear that addressing the challenges posed by ego and arrogance requires a multifaceted approach that touches every aspect of human life and society. The path ahead is complex but rich with potential for transformative change and collective flourishing.

Synthesis of Key Themes:

1. <u>Personal Transformation:</u> The journey begins with individual growth, cultivating self-awareness, humility, and compassion. This inner work forms the foundation for all other changes.

2. <u>Interpersonal Dynamics:</u> We can create more harmonious and productive relationships by fostering empathy, authentic communication, and collaborative skills.

3. <u>Organizational Change:</u> Reimagining leadership and institutional structures can align our collective efforts with values of humility, service, and shared prosperity.

4. <u>Societal Shifts:</u> Addressing systemic issues and cultural narratives is crucial for creating a societal context that supports rather than hinders personal and collective growth.

5. <u>Global Perspectives:</u> In our interconnected world, fostering a sense of global citizenship and cooperation is essential for addressing shared challenges.

6. <u>Technological Ethics:</u> Ensuring our technological future aligns with human values requires ongoing ethical reflection and proactive governance.

7. <u>Environmental Stewardship:</u> Cultivating a sustainable relationship with our planet is not just an ecological imperative but a spiritual and ethical one.

8. <u>Education and Lifelong Learning:</u> Preparing for an uncertain future demands reimagining education to foster adaptability,

critical thinking, and a love of learning.

9. <u>Spiritual and Philosophical Integration:</u> Finding meaning and purpose in a complex world requires integrating diverse wisdom traditions with contemporary knowledge.

The Way Forward:

<u>The path ahead requires us to embrace several key principles:</u>

1. **<u>Humility:</u>** Recognizing our individual and collective limitations while remaining open to growth and learning.

2. **<u>Interconnectedness:</u>** Understanding that our fates are inextricably linked, from the personal to the planetary level.

3. **<u>Balance:</u>** Finding equilibrium between individual agency and collective responsibility, tradition and innovation, local action and global thinking.

4. **<u>Adaptability:</u>** Cultivating the flexibility to navigate rapid change while maintaining core values and purpose.

5. **<u>Integration:</u>** Bringing together diverse perspectives, disciplines, and ways of knowing to address complex challenges.

6. **<u>Long-term Thinking</u>**: Extending our consideration to future generations and the long-term consequences of our actions.

7. **<u>Compassionate Action:</u>** Combining deep care for others with practical, effective efforts to create positive change.

<u>Challenges and Opportunities:</u>

The road ahead is with obstacles. Entrenched systems, deeply ingrained habits, and the sheer complexity of global issues present challenges. However, these challenges also present opportunities for innovation, collaboration, and profound transformation.

Some key challenges include:

- Overcoming short-term thinking in politics and business

- Bridging ideological divides and fostering genuine dialogue

- Ensuring that technological progress serves human and ecological well-being

- Addressing global inequalities while respecting cultural diversity

- Maintaining hope and motivation in the face of daunting global issues

Yet, we also see promising developments:

- Growing awareness of global challenges and interconnectedness

- Emerging technologies that can support sustainable development and global cooperation

- Increasing recognition of the importance of emotional intelligence and soft skills

- Rising movements for social and environmental justice

- Renewed interest in contemplative practices and holistic well-being

Call to Action:

Moving forward requires commitment and action at all levels:

1. **Individual:** Engage in personal growth practices, cultivate self-awareness, and make conscious choices aligned with

broader well-being.

2. **Community:** Foster local initiatives that build connection, resilience, and shared purpose.

3. **Organizational:** Implement ethical leadership practices and structures that support collective flourishing.

4. **National:** Advocate for policies prioritising long-term well-being, sustainability, and social justice.

5. **Global:** Take part in and support international cooperation and understanding efforts.

The journey beyond ego and arrogance is not a destination but an ongoing process of growth and refinement. It calls us to continually expand our circles of compassion, deepen our understanding, and align our actions with our highest values.

As we face the complexities of our time, let us remember that our greatest strength lies not in individual brilliance or achievement but in our ability for collective wisdom, mutual support, and shared purpose. By embracing humility and fostering genuine connection - with ourselves, each other, and the world around us - we open the door to transformative possibilities for our shared future.

The path forward is not always easy, but it is one we must walk together. With courage, compassion, and commitment, we can create a world that transcends the limitations of ego and arrogance and embodies the profound potential of human wisdom and love.

Applying Biblical Wisdom to Modern Challenges

Throughout our exploration of the way forward, we can

draw significant insights from biblical wisdom to address contemporary issues:

1. Humility and Servant Leadership:

- The biblical concept of servant leadership, exemplified by Jesus washing his disciples' feet (John 13:1-17), offers a powerful organisational and political leadership model.

- Proverbs 11:2 reminds us that "When pride comes, then comes disgrace, but with humility comes wisdom," emphasising the importance of humility in personal and societal growth.

2. Stewardship and Environmental Care:

- The biblical mandate to be stewards of the Earth (Genesis 1:28, 2:15) provides a strong foundation for environmental ethics and sustainable practices.

3. Social Justice and Equality:

- Prophetic traditions of speaking truth to power and advocating for the marginalised (e.g., Amos 5:24) can inspire modern movements for social justice.

The concept that all humans are created in God's image (Genesis 1:27) underpins notions of universal human dignity and rights.

4. Community and Interconnectedness:

- The metaphor of the body of Christ (1 Corinthians 12:12-27) offers a powerful model for understanding human interconnectedness and the value of diversity.

5. Ethical Technology Use:

- While the Bible does not directly address

modern technology, principles like using one's talents responsibly (Matthew 25:14-30) can guide ethical technology development and use.

6. **Conflict Resolution and Peacemaking:**

   - Jesus' teachings on reconciliation and loving one's enemies (Matthew 5:9, 5:43-48) guide addressing global conflicts and fostering international cooperation.

7. **Holistic Education:**

   - The biblical emphasis on wisdom that goes beyond mere knowledge (Proverbs 4:7) can inform approaches to education that cultivate skills, character, and discernment.

8. **Balancing Work and Rest:**

   - The concept of Sabbath (Exodus 20:8-11) offers wisdom for addressing work-life balance and burnout issues in modern society.

By integrating these biblical insights with contemporary knowledge and diverse perspectives, we can develop more holistic and ethically grounded approaches to our challenges. This integration allows us to draw on timeless wisdom while staying responsive to the unique contexts of our modern world.

CHAPTER 10: PROGRAMMED OBSOLESCENCE: THE EGO OF ENDLESS CONSUMPTION

1. Introduction: The Hidden Strategy of Disposability

In our exploration of ego and arrogance in modern society, we now focus on a practice that embodies the intersection of corporate greed, environmental disregard, and consumer manipulation: programmed obsolescence. This strategy, where products are deliberately designed to become outdated or non-functional after a certain period, reflects a profound arrogance in our approach to resources, technology, and human needs.

2. Understanding Programmed Obsolescence

Programmed obsolescence, also known as planned obsolescence, is a business strategy in which a product's obsolescence (becoming obsolete) is planned and built into it from its conception. This may involve:

a) Designing a product to break down or wear out at a

particular time (I.e. counterfeit products)

b) Continually updating the appearance or design of a product, making older versions seem undesirable (I.e. mobile phone and/or their operating system)

c) Stopping the production of replacement parts (i.e. car parts)

d) Creating software that slows down older hardware (i.e. Microsoft and Apple)

This practice spans various industries, from electronics and appliances to fashion and automobiles.

3. Historical Context and Evolution

The concept of programmed obsolescence gained prominence in the 1920s and 1930s, seen as a way to stimulate consumer demand during the Great Depression. It became more widespread in the post-World War II era, coinciding with the rise of consumer culture.

4. The Ego of Industry: Profit Over Sustainability

The drive for continual growth and profit maximisation reflects a corporate ego that places short-term gains over long-term sustainability. This mindset aligns with the biblical warning: "For the love of money is a root of all kinds of evil" (1 Timothy 6:10).

5. Consumer Psychology and the Cult of the New

Programmed obsolescence exploits human desires for status and novelty. This reflects the "lust of the eyes and pride of life" that the apostle John warns against (1 John 2:16), highlighting how our egos can make us susceptible to manipulation.

6. Environmental Impact: The Arrogance of Waste

The environmental consequences of programmed obsolescence are severe, contributing to resource depletion and growing waste. This practice starkly contrasts the biblical principle of stewardship, where humans are called to be responsible caretakers of the Earth (Genesis 2:15).

7. Technological Implications: Innovation vs. Incremental Changes

While companies often justify programmed obsolescence as driving innovation, it frequently results in minor, unnecessary changes rather than significant advancements. This reflects a failure to use our God-given creativity responsibly (Exodus 35:31-32).

8. Legal and Ethical Considerations

Some countries have begun implementing laws against programmed obsolescence, recognising it as a deceptive practice. From a biblical perspective, this aligns with the call for honest business practices (Proverbs 11:1).

9. The Right to Repair Movement

The Right to Repair movement has emerged in response to programmed obsolescence, advocating for consumers' ability to repair and modify their devices. This movement embodies principles of stewardship and self-reliance that resonate with biblical values.

10. Alternative Business Models: Durability and Circular Economy

Some companies are embracing alternative models focused on durability and repairability. The circular economy concept, emphasising reuse and recycling, aligns more closely with biblical principles of stewardship and resourcefulness.

11. Consumer Responsibility and Mindful Consumption

Consumers play a crucial role in combating programmed obsolescence through mindful purchasing decisions. This aligns with the biblical call for wisdom and discernment in all aspects of life (Proverbs 4:7).

12. Technological Solutions: Modular Design and Software Support

Innovations in modular design and extended software support offer technical solutions to programmed obsolescence, demonstrating how human ingenuity can be used responsibly.

13. Policy Recommendations: Towards Sustainable Production

Effective policies can encourage longer product lifespans and more sustainable production methods. This reflects the biblical principle that those in authority must enact just laws (Romans 13:1-7).

14. Biblical Wisdom for a Sustainable Future

The Bible offers timeless wisdom that can guide us towards more sustainable practices:

- Stewardship: "The earth is the Lord's, and everything in it" (Psalm 24:1)

- Contentment: "Keep your lives free from the love of money and be content with what you have" (Hebrews 13:5)

- Responsibility: "Whatever you do, work at it with all your heart, as working for the Lord" (Colossians 3:23)

15. Conclusion: From Obsolescence to Timeless Value

Overcoming programmed obsolescence requires a fundamental value shift from short-term gratification to long-term stewardship. By embracing biblical principles of responsible stewardship, ethical business practices, and contentment, we can move towards a more sustainable and fulfilling approach to production and consumption.

As we conclude, let us remember the words of Jesus: "Do not store up for yourselves treasures on earth, where moths and vermin destroy, and where thieves break in and steal. But store up for yourselves treasures in heaven" (Matthew 6:19-20). In our material pursuits, may we seek lasting value and purpose, rejecting the ego-driven cycle of endless consumption in favour of a more balanced, sustainable, and spiritually grounded way of life.

CHAPTER 11:
THE EGO'S WEB:
UNTANGLING THE
SELF IN MODERN
SOCIETY

1. Introduction: The Pervasive Influence of Ego

A common thread appears as we've journeyed through the myriad manifestations of ego and arrogance in our modern world - from politics and healthcare to consumerism and technology. The ego, that sense of self that distinguishes "I" from "other," plays a pivotal role in shaping our societal structures, our perception of ourselves, and our place in the world. This chapter will explore how the themes discussed throughout this book intersect with fundamental aspects of human psychology and behaviour, particularly self-worth, beauty, self-image, self-values, self-ethic, self-reliance, and co-dependency.

2. The Ego's Mirror: Self-Worth and Self-Image in the Age of Arrogance

Our exploration of consumerism and advertising (Chapters

4 and 7) uncovered how modern marketing tactics often prey on insecurities to drive consumption. This constant bombardment of idealised images and lifestyles has profound implications for self-worth and self-image.

The biblical perspective reminds us that our worth is inherent, stemming from being created in God's image (Genesis 1:27). Yet, in a world that often measures value by external metrics - wealth, status, appearance - many struggle with a distorted sense of self-worth.

The rise of social media, as discussed in our discussion of technology (Chapter 5), has amplified these issues. The curated versions of life presented online can lead to constant comparison, often detrimental to self-image. The biblical call to find our identity in Christ (Galatians 2:20) offers a counterpoint to this external validation-seeking behaviour.

3. Beauty and the Beast of Ego

The concept of beauty, particularly concerning self-image, is deeply intertwined with the ego's need for validation. Our examination of the healthcare industry (Chapter 3) touched on the rise of cosmetic procedures, reflecting a societal obsession with physical appearance often driven by ego and insecurity.

The biblical perspective on beauty emphasises inner qualities over outward appearance (1 Peter 3:3-4). This wisdom provides a powerful antidote to the ego's relentless pursuit of an often unattainable physical ideal.

4. Self-Values in a World of Shifting Sands

Throughout our exploration, particularly in discussions of politics (Chapter 2) and business ethics, we've seen how ego-driven pursuits of power and wealth can distort societal values. This macro-level shift has implications for individual self-values.

In a world where success is often defined by material wealth or social status, many struggle to maintain values aligned with more profound spiritual or ethical principles. The biblical emphasis on storing "treasures in heaven" (Matthew 6:20) provides a framework for developing self-values that transcend worldly measures of success.

5. The Self-Ethic: Navigating Moral Choices in an Ego-Driven World

Our discussions of ethical challenges in various sectors—from healthcare to technology to business—highlight the importance of a strong personal ethical framework. Self-ethics, or one's internal moral compass, is constantly challenged in a world where ego-driven behaviours are often rewarded.

The biblical call to "do justice, love kindness, and walk humbly with your God" (Micah 6:8) offers a foundation for developing a self-ethic that resists the allure of ego-driven moral compromises.

6. Self-Reliance and the Illusion of Independence

While the American ideal of self-reliance is often seen as a virtue, it can become problematic when taken to ego-driven extremes. Our exploration of programmed obsolescence (Chapter 10) touched on how this mindset can lead to unsustainable consumption patterns.

From a biblical perspective, genuine self-reliance is paradoxically rooted in dependence on God (Proverbs 3:5-6). This understanding can help balance healthy self-reliance with an awareness of our interconnectedness and need for community.

7. Co-dependency: The Shadow Side of Ego

While much of our discussion has focused on the overt manifestations of ego, it's crucial to recognise that ego-driven behaviour can manifest as co-dependency. This pattern, where one's sense of self is excessively tied to others' approval or needs, is another form of ego distortion.

Our examination of interpersonal dynamics and organisational structures shows how codependent behaviours can emerge in various contexts. The biblical call to "speak the truth in love" (Ephesians 4:15) guides the development of healthier, more balanced relationships.

8. The Ego in the Digital Age: Technology and the Self

Our discussion of AI and technology (Chapter 5) highlighted how digital environments can become extensions of the ego. Social media profiles, virtual realities, and online personas can all become arenas for ego expression and validation-seeking.

The challenge in this digital age is maintaining a grounded sense of self rooted in real-world values and relationships. The biblical wisdom of being "in the world but not of the world" (John 17:14-15) takes on new relevance in navigating our digital existence.

9. Transcending the Ego: Lessons from Spiritual Wisdom

Throughout this book, we have drawn on biblical wisdom to counter ego-driven behaviours. The consistent message across spiritual traditions is the need to transcend the limited, ego-bound self to connect with a deeper, more universal reality.

Practices like prayer, meditation, and selfless service, emphasised in biblical teachings, offer practical ways to loosen the ego's grip on our sense of self and behaviour.

10. Towards an Integrated Self: Balancing Ego and Humility

The goal is not to cut the ego—it serves essential functions in human psychology—but to right-size it. An integrated self-recognises the ego's role while not being enslaved to its demands for validation and superiority.

This balance is beautifully captured in Jesus' teaching to "love your neighbour as yourself" (Mark 12:31). It acknowledges the importance of self-love (a healthy ego) while extending that same regard to others (transcending ego-centricity).

11. The Ego and Societal Structures: A Cyclical Relationship

As we've explored throughout this book, the manifestation of ego in individual psychology is both shaped by and shapes our societal structures. This cyclical relationship creates a self-reinforcing system that can be challenging to break.

For instance, our discussion of politics and power (Chapter 2) revealed how political systems often reward ego-driven behaviours, which in turn perpetuate those very systems. Similarly, in our examination of consumerism (Chapter 4), we saw how marketing strategies exploit individual insecurities, fueling a cycle of consumption that further entrenches these insecurities.

Understanding this cyclical relationship is crucial for both personal growth and societal change. The biblical call to be "transformed by renewing your mind" (Romans 12:2) becomes more significant when we recognise that individual transformation can catalyse broader societal shifts.

12. The Ego and Professional Identity

Our exploration of various professional sectors - healthcare, technology, pharmaceuticals - highlighted how ego can intertwine with professional identity. This intersection can lead to both positive and negative outcomes.

A healthy sense of professional pride can drive excellence and innovation. Conversely, over-identifying one's professional role can lead to arrogance, resistance to change, and ethical blind spots.

The biblical concept of vocation - seeing one's work as a calling rather than merely a career - offers a framework for developing a professional identity that transcends ego-driven motivations. This perspective aligns with the idea of work as service, as exemplified in Colossians 3:23: "Whatever you do, work at it with all your heart, as working for the Lord, not for human masters."

13. The Ego and Generational Dynamics

Our changing world, with its rapid technological advancements and shifting social norms, has created unique generational dynamics that intersect with issues of ego and self-perception.

Older generations may struggle with feelings of irrelevance in a fast-changing world, potentially leading to ego-defensive behaviours. Younger generations, growing up in an era of social media and personal branding, face unprecedented pressures to curate and promote their personal image.

The wisdom literature of the Bible, with its emphasis on respecting elders while valuing the energy and insight of youth, provides a balanced perspective on navigating these generational dynamics.

14. The Ego and Global Challenges

As discussed in our chapters on environmental stewardship and global perspectives (Chapters 6 and 9), many of the world's most pressing challenges—climate change, inequality, conflict—can be traced back to ego-driven behaviours on both individual and collective levels.

Addressing these global issues requires a shift from ego-centric thinking to a more holistic, interconnected worldview. The biblical concept of stewardship, which extends beyond individual concerns to encompass care for all creation, offers a model for this expanded perspective.

15. The Ego and Spiritual Life

While we've drawn on biblical wisdom throughout this book, it's worth exploring how the ego interacts with spiritual life more deeply. Paradoxically, even pursuing spiritual growth can become an ego-driven endeavour, leading to spiritual pride or using spirituality to self-aggrandise.

The biblical warnings against hypocrisy and performing righteous acts for public approval (Matthew 6:1) speak directly to this tendency. From this perspective, proper spiritual growth involves a continual surrender of the ego to a higher purpose.

16. Practical Strategies for Ego Management

Having explored the many facets of the ego's influence, offering practical strategies for managing and right-sizing the ego daily is crucial. These might include:

- Mindfulness practices to increase self-awareness

- Gratitude exercises to counteract ego-driven entitlement

- Service activities to shift focus from self to others

- Regular self-reflection and moral inventory

- Seeking feedback and practising humility in relationships

These practices align with many biblical teachings and can help foster a healthier relationship with one's ego.

17. The Ego and Human Potential

While much of our discussion has focused on the problematic aspects of ego, it's essential to recognise that a healthy ego is vital for human functioning and achievement. The key is finding the balance between a robust sense of self and the humility to acknowledge one's place in a larger context.

This balanced perspective allows for the full expression of human potential, not in service of self-aggrandisement but in service of a greater good. It aligns with the biblical idea of humans as co-creators with God, using our gifts and talents to contribute positively to the world.

18. Moving Forwards: Towards an Ego-Aware Society

As we conclude this expansive exploration of the ego's role in modern society, we are left with both a challenge and an opportunity. The challenge is to recognise and mitigate the negative impacts of unchecked ego across all spheres of life. The opportunity is to harness our understanding of ego to create more conscious, compassionate, and sustainable ways of living and organising our world.

By cultivating ego awareness on both individual and collective levels, we can create a society that balances healthy self-esteem with genuine care for others and our shared environment. This vision aligns closely with the biblical concept of shalom, a holistic peace encompassing the right relationships with self, others, creation, and the divine.

In striving towards this ego-aware society, we have the potential to address the root causes of many of our most pressing issues, from personal psychological struggles to global existential threats. This journey requires ongoing commitment, compassion, and courage, but it promises a more fulfilling, just, and sustainable future for all.

19. Conclusion: The Path to Authentic Selfhood

As we have seen throughout this book, ego and arrogance permeate our society, from our political and economic systems to our relationships and self-perceptions. The path forward involves a dual movement: an honest recognition of the ego's influence in our lives and a concerted effort to align our sense of self with deeper values and universal truths.

By understanding the ego's web—its effects on our sense of worth, perception of beauty, values, ethics, relationships, and behaviour—we can untangle ourselves from its limiting influences. In doing so, we can live more authentically, compassionately, and in harmony with our deepest selves and the world around us.

The biblical promise that "the truth will set you free" (John 8:32) takes on profound significance in this context. As we free ourselves from the distortions of an overinflated ego, we move toward a more authentic, more integrated sense of self—one capable of navigating the complexities of modern life with wisdom, compassion, and grace.

CONCLUSION: HUMILITY, WISDOM, AND THE PATH FORWARD

As we conclude our exploration of ego and arrogance in modern society, we find ourselves at a critical juncture. Our challenges are complex and multifaceted, touching every aspect of human life, from the personal to the global. Yet, throughout our journey, we have found that ancient wisdom, notably in biblical teachings, offers profound guidance for navigating these modern challenges.

Synthesis of Key Themes:

1. The Nature of Ego and Arrogance (Chapter 1):

We began by examining the roots of ego and arrogance in human nature. The biblical perspective reminds us of humanity's fallen nature (Romans 3:23) and the constant struggle against pride. As Proverbs 16:18 warns, "Pride goes before destruction, a haughty spirit before a fall." This understanding forms the foundation for our approach to addressing ego-driven behaviours in various spheres of life.

2. Politics and Power (Chapter 2):

In exploring politics and power, we saw how the biblical model of servant leadership, exemplified by Jesus washing his disciples' feet (John 13:1-17), offers a powerful antidote to the ego-driven pursuit of power. The prophet Micah's call to "act justly, love mercy and walk humbly with your God" (Micah 6:8) provides a timeless guideline for ethical leadership.

3. Healthcare (Chapter 3):

Our examination of healthcare revealed the tension between service and industry. The biblical emphasis on compassion and healing, as demonstrated throughout Jesus' ministry, reminds us of the core purpose of healthcare. The parable of the Good Samaritan (Luke 10:25-37) continues to inspire a model of care that transcends social boundaries and self-interest.

4. Consumerism and the Cult of Self (Chapter 4):

Jesus' teachings on the dangers of materialism provide guidance in addressing the challenges of consumerism. His words, "You cannot serve both God and money" (Matthew 6:24), call us to examine our priorities and find fulfilment beyond material possessions.

5. Artificial Intelligence and Technology (Chapter 5):

While the Bible doesn't directly address modern technology, principles of stewardship and using one's talents responsibly (Matthew 25:14-30) provide a framework for ethical technology development and use. The wisdom literature's emphasis on discernment (Proverbs 2:3-5) is particularly relevant in navigating the complexities of AI ethics.

6. Pharmaceutical Industry (Chapter 6):

Examining the pharmaceutical industry reminded us of the biblical call to heal and care for the sick (Matthew 10:8). This divine mandate challenges us to balance profit motives with the ethical imperative to promote health and well-being for all.

7. Advertising and Manipulation (Chapter 7):

Our exploration of advertising brought to light the biblical warnings against deception and the manipulation of others. The call to "speak the truth in love" (Ephesians 4:15) provides an ethical standard for communication that respects human dignity.

8. Prophecy and Warnings (Chapter 8):

The biblical prophetic tradition offers a model for addressing societal issues with courage and foresight. Like the prophets of old, we are called to speak truth to power and advocate for justice while maintaining humility and dependence on divine guidance.

9. The Way Forward (Chapter 9):

In charting the path forward, we find inspiration in the biblical vision of shalom - a holistic peace encompassing the right relationships with God, others, and creation. The transformative power of love, as described in 1 Corinthians 13, provides a foundation for personal and societal change.

Biblical Principles for the Path Forward:

1. **Humility:** Recognizing our limitations and dependence on God and others. "God opposes the proud but favours the humble" (James 4:6).

2. **Love and Compassion:** Extending care beyond our immediate circle to embrace all of humanity and creation. "Love your neighbour as yourself" (Mark 12:31).

3. **Justice and Equity:** Working towards a society that

reflects God's concern for the marginalised. "Defend the weak and the fatherless; uphold the cause of the poor and the oppressed" (Psalm 82:3).

4. **Stewardship:** Responsibly managing resources, technology, and the environment as gifts entrusted to us by God. "The earth is the Lord's, and everything in it" (Psalm 24:1).

5. **Wisdom and Discernment:** Seeking deeper understanding and applying it ethically. "The fear of the Lord is the beginning of wisdom" (Proverbs 9:10).

6. **Community and Interconnectedness:** Recognizing our fundamental unity and interdependence. "For just as each of us has one body with many members...so in Christ we, though many, form one body" (Romans 12:4-5).

7. **Redemption and Transformation:** Believing in the possibility of positive change, both personal and societal. "Do not conform to the pattern of this world, but be transformed by renewing your mind" (Romans 12:2).

8. **Sustainable Stewardship:** Embracing a long-term, responsible resource use and production approach. "The earth is the Lord's, and everything in it" (Psalm 24:1).

10. **Programmed Obsolescence:** The Ego of Endless Consumption (Chapter 10): Our examination of programmed obsolescence revealed a practice that embodies corporate greed, environmental disregard, and consumer manipulation. This strategy reflects a profound arrogance in our approach to resources and human needs. The biblical principles of stewardship (Genesis 2:15) and contentment (Hebrews 13:5) offer a powerful counternarrative to the culture of endless consumption. Jesus' warning against storing treasures on earth (Matthew 6:19-20) challenges us to seek lasting value beyond material possessions.

11. **The Ego's Web:** Untangling the Self in Modern Society (Chapter 11): Our final exploration delved deep into the pervasive influence of ego across all aspects of modern life, tying together the threads from our previous discussions. We examined how ego and arrogance profoundly affect our sense of self-worth, perception of beauty, values, ethics, and relationships. The chapter highlighted the cyclical relationship between individual ego and societal structures, showing how personal transformation can catalyse broader societal change.

As we face the complex challenges of our time—from environmental crises to technological disruptions, from social inequalities to ethical dilemmas in various industries—these biblical principles offer a compass for navigation. They remind us that the antidote to ego and arrogance lies not in mere behavioural modification but in a fundamental reorientation of heart and mind toward humility, love, and service.

The way forward requires integrating this timeless wisdom with contemporary knowledge and diverse perspectives. It calls for courage to challenge ego-driven systems, compassion to heal divisions, and creativity to imagine new possibilities. Above all, it demands recognition of our shared humanity and collective responsibility as stewards of God's creation.

As we conclude, let us heed the words of the prophet Micah, which encapsulate the essence of our journey beyond ego and arrogance: "And what does the Lord require of you? To act justly and to love mercy and to walk humbly with your God" (Micah 6:8). In this spirit of humble service, guided by divine wisdom and motivated by love, we can work towards a future that reflects not the limitations of human ego, but the boundless potential of a humanity aligned with its highest calling.

May we renew our commitment to stewardship, justice,

and compassion? We reject the ego-driven cycles of powe
consumption, and obsolescence in favour of a more balanced
sustainable, and spiritually grounded way of life. In doing so,
we address the challenges of our time and honour our divine
calling as caretakers of creation and servants of one another.

333